D0712761

AURARIA

GOLD DIGGERS

AURARIA

THE STORY OF
A GEORGIA GOLD-MINING TOWN

E. MERTON COULTER

THE UNIVERSITY OF GEORGIA PRESS
ATHENS

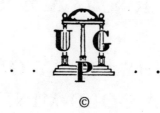

©

COPYRIGHT 1956

THE UNIVERSITY OF GEORGIA PRESS

Library of Congress Catalog Number 56-13005

Printed in the United States of America

CONTENTS

ILLUSTRATIONS

These illustrations with the exception of those on pages 34 and 75 first appeared in "Gold Mining in Georgia," *Harper's New Monthly Magazine,* LIX (1879).

PREFACE

THIS book was made possible by the discovery and use of a complete file of the *Western Herald,* a newspaper published in Auraria. True enough, the paper lasted for slightly less than a year, but it was during this early period that Auraria grew up and reached its zenith as a gold-mining town. The *Western Herald* as a basic source, together with various supplementary material, has afforded a close-up view of an exciting period of gold-mining history in the South, antedating by almost two decades the mining booms in the West.

Though there is no attempt here to give a history of gold-mining in the South or even in Georgia, the importance of this book goes far beyond a mere local study. Apart from its description of life in a booming and exciting gold-mining town, the first in American history, this book in placing Auraria in its proper perspective, brings in historic developments which concerned the South and the nation as a whole. Political and constitutional issues break out in the states rights and unionism doctrines incident to the Nullification controversy, in the United States Supreme Court decisions relative to the removal of the Cherokee Indians, and in the clash of the personalities of John C. Calhoun and Andrew Jackson; a touch of finance and economics appears in banks, mints, private coinage, and turnpikes; social history is seen in religion, education, patriotic celebrations, dances, and chuck-a-luck games and other forms of gambling; and some literary activities are noted in the coming and going of newspapers and in a flash or two of Mark Twain and William Gilmore Simms.

The story of Auraria is a little epic in itself: the unforgettable character of Grandma Paschal, who clung to Auraria to the end, while a son and other Aurarians went to Texas to fight for its independence and to stay there and become important in that state's history; the small band of Aurarians who found gold on Cherry Creek in the eastern foothills of the Rockies and ushered in the Pike's Peak gold rush and the founding of their little transplanted Auraria in the West, which soon was to become the city of Denver; and Auraria in Georgia dwindling and fading out until in the twentieth century it could well qualify as one of the dead towns, which, like the dead towns of the West, came to be a sentimental link with the past.

Here is history both from the grass-roots and from the mountain tops.

E. MERTON COULTER

GOLD IN THE HILLS

THERE'S millions in it," was an expression made famous by Mark Twain in his *Guilded Age,* but it was not coined by Mark. Nor was it coined by William Sellers, from whom Mark got it and whom he thought to honor by putting him and his expression in the book — in a later edition he changed the name to Mulberry Sellers on William's objection to being so honored. This expression was in fact uttered and reuttered by a Lumpkin County Georgian, Dr. Matthew F. Stephenson, in 1849, as he pointed to a ridge flecked with gold, in his efforts to dissuade his neighbors from stampeding to the gold mines of California.[1] It soon came to be corrupted in that same North Georgia region, into "Thar's gold in them thar hills."

How far back in time people knew that there was gold in the Georgia hills, is a matter of speculation. Hernando de Soto suspected it and marched somewhere in the vicinity of North Georgia looking for it, inspired in his search by the Indians, who hurried him along to get rid of him and his brigands. It stands to reason that the Indians, who knew what gold was, had been finding shining particles of it from time out of mind; but they were not finding it in sufficient quantities to make any use of it, and, in fact, they were not looking for it. They had rather hunt the deer that infested the country, fight neighboring tribes, and let their squaws scratch the surface of the old fields to induce the growth of a little stunted corn and more vigorous squashes.

But about 1828 or 1829, things began to happen. Although previously, according to vague rumors, the Indians had found some gold nuggets or small particles of the shining metal, not until now did news begin to flash as quickly as gossip could spread it, that gold had been discovered in Northeast Georgia on the land of the Cherokee Indians. The exact spot and the identity of the finder are obscure, as, indeed, are the exact month and year. But Benjamin Parks, in 1894, at the age of 94, remembered that early in 1828, while he was out deer hunting he kicked up something which caught his eye. He examined it and concluded that it was gold. Soon the news got out, and in his words, "such excitement you never saw. It seemed, within a few days, as if the whole world must have heard of it; for men came from every State, I had ever heard of. They came afoot, on horseback, and in wagons, acting more like crazy men than anything else." They were soon "panning out of the branches, and making holes in the hillsides."[2]

Complications immediately arose. The Cherokees claimed all northern Georgia as their own independent nation and they strongly objected to this invasion by hordes of white men. The United States government, which recognized through various treaties the rights of the Cherokees to this region, immediately became interested, and to protect the Indians it sent in Federal troops to patrol the mines and try to preserve order. But most concerned of all was Georgia, within whose bounds all this furor was taking place; for years before, in 1802, the Federal government had promised the state that all of the Indians would be removed from her limits. In 1828, about the time the gold fever broke out, Georgia, tired of waiting on the tardy fulfillment of a promise now more than a quarter of century old, decided to cut the Gordian knot. The legislature sliced up the whole Chero-

kee Nation and added it to the five most northern counties —
Carroll, DeKalb, Gwinnett, Hall, and Habersham. Also it
declared that "all white persons residing" among the Cherokees were now subject to the laws of the state and that after
June 1, 1830 all Indians should come under such laws and
regulations as the legislature might thereafter prescribe.[3]
Georgia was now on the highroad to driving the Indians
beyond the Mississippi. In 1829, it imposed penalties against
anyone who tried to discourage or impede the Indians from
migrating, and it denied the right of any Indian to be a wit-
ness in any suit to which a white man was a party, unless the
white man was a resident of the Cherokee nation.[4] And the
next year (1830) Georgia went the full distance in suppressing the Cherokee nation short of expelling the Indians. All
tribal organizations and councils were forbidden to meet and
all functions, laws, and customs were made null and void.
The intruding white men were also to be brought more completely under the supremacy of the state. Any such person
in the Indian country after March 1, 1831 must have a license
or permit to reside there and before he could secure such
permit he must take an oath to support the constitution of
Georgia.[5]

For a decade and more, missionaries had been working
among the Cherokees, bringing to them the white man's
religion and civilization, but more particularly strengthening
the resolve of the Indians not to move. When Samuel
Worcester, a missionary from Massachusetts, and others in-
dignantly refused to accept permits from the despised au-
thorities of Georgia, they were arrested, tried, and sentenced
to the penitentiary; but all except Worcester and one other
accepted pardons and were freed. Worcester, now in 1832,
was determined to force the case into the United States Supreme Court, where he expected to have a decision declaring
null and void Georgia's laws regarding the Cherokee nation
(a decision that the Court had not been able to make in the
case of Cherokee Nation *vs.* Georgia decided the previous

year). Worcester would, of course, then receive his freedom. Worcester had guessed right; the Court declared Georgia's laws unconstitutional; but the state paid not the slightest attention to this decision except to denounce it. And President Andrew Jackson, who had grown famous fighting Indians, Britishers, and Tories, let it be known that he intended to let patriotic Georgia have her own way.

As the presence of Federal troops in Georgia was distasteful to the state, Jackson obligingly withdrew them. For the consolidation of her authority in the Cherokee country, and especially for "the protection of the mines," Georgia in 1830 authorized the governor to enlist a force of men to be known as the Georgia Guards. They were to be organized as foot soldiers or cavalrymen, "as the occasion may require," and to number not more than sixty. To secure their proper discipline, the commander was allowed three sergeants and was given permission to dismiss at any time anyone guilty of "disorderly conduct." The Guards were permitted to arrest anyone charged with violating the laws of the state and to convey such person to the nearest justice of the peace or judge, for trial.[6]

While Georgia was thus laying hold of the Cherokee country, suppressing the Indian government, and trying to drive out the Indians, the great "intrusion" of hordes of whites was in full swing. Who could stop it? The Federal troops had been withdrawn in 1830, and sixty Georgia Guards could hardly succeed where the departing army had failed. Before leaving, a major in the United States forces described a heterogeneous group of intruders at one spot in the heart of the gold region. Estimating their number at more than two hundred, he declared that they "presented a most motley appearance of whites, Indians, halfbreeds and negroes, boys of fourteen and old men of seventy — and indeed their occupations appeared to be as various as their complexions comprising diggers, sawyers, shopkeepers, pedlars, thieves and gamblers, etc. besides them were also found in the hopeful

assemblage two colonels of Georgia Militia, two candidates
for the legislature and two ministers of the Gospel, all no
doubt attracted thither by the love of gold."[7]

These intruders had no right to be here at this time and
after March 1 of 1831 they had to have written permits if
they should be found in this region. In the first place, the
land, by treaty right, belonged to the Indians and in theory
it continued to belong to them until 1835, when they signed
a treaty with the United States to go beyond the Mississippi.
However, when Georgia extended her authority over the
Cherokee nation, she assumed the ownership of the land, but
with the announced understanding that the Indians should
be paid for all of their improvements.

To set the land-hungry Georgians down on this region, the
state used the land lottery system, which it had devised in
1803 for the disposal of its great public domain. This system
gave every citizen of the state meeting certain qualifications
one chance or draw, with an additional draw to certain favored classes, as, for instance, the heads of families or Revolutionary soldiers. A family of orphans was counted as a citizen
and entitled to one draw. The Cherokee country was now
divided into 160-acre lots, except for the gold region, which
was reduced to 40-acre lots. Preparatory to settling the people on the Cherokee lands, Georgia in 1830 re-assembled the
slices of the Cherokee nation which she had given in 1828 to
the five northern counties, and now made them into one
county to be called Cherokee.[8]

The Cherokee lottery began in the fall of 1832 and was
completed by the early part of May following.[9] But of course,
in the meanwhile there had been a great deal of illegal digging, for the ownership of the land was not settled until the
lottery was held. And in addition to this confusion there
were the frauds worked in the lottery by those who exercised
more draws than they were entitled to. In fact some Georgians from the beginning had been opposed to the lottery
system of disposing of the state's patrimony. And now, when

the Cherokee lottery had been completed, one of the sharpest attacks was made against it by a resident of the gold region. "Thus has the State of Georgia continued from year to year," he said, "to gamble away her rich inheritance. It is indeed painful for one who feels as a Georgian should, to contrast Georgia as she is, with Georgia as she might have been. Her immense extent of territory which might have been so appropriated, as to have filled our whole state with the most splendid works of improvement — might have afforded employment to thousands of her citizens, and thus have filled their barns and storehouses, with plenty — might have forever dispensed with the necessity of taxing her citizens — might have been a resort to the oppressed and enterprising of all nations, and have stood forth, the pride of her people, for the emulous admiration for her sister states. But alas for her, her Legislatures have listened to the siren song of gaming, and the State of Georgia has disgracefully infatuated, literally and emphatically, gambled away her rich inheritance, and must sooner or later, feel through every member of her political body, the effect of her misguided legislation, and the infatuated spirit of her policy."[10]

The main gold deposits of Georgia extended through her hills and mountains from the northeastern corner of the state southwestwardly to the Alabama line.[11] Their greatest richness lay in an area about forty miles west of the Savannah River and an equal distance south of the North Carolina line, and here was where the first big discovery had been made in 1828. After the suppression of the Cherokee Nation, this region had first been made a part of Hall and Habersham counties and then included in Cherokee County; but in December 1832, it was erected into Lumpkin County. At the same time the remainder of Cherokee County was cut into nine counties, one of which retained the name Cherokee. The first wild swarm of intruders settled on a ridge between the Chestatee and Etowah rivers, which were only two miles apart at this point — a sort of roof of this part of the world it was, for though both rivers flowed southward here, soon the Etowah continued westward to enter the Coosa and on into the Alabama and finally to reach the Gulf of Mexico at Mobile, while the Chestatee continued on southward to join the Chattahoochee and flow into the Gulf at Apalachicola on the coast of Florida.

This was a strategic spot on which to congregate, for the easiest way to mine gold here was to wash out the sand and gravel in the streams and on bottom lands — the so-called placer mining. With spade and pan and rocker cradles the miners began to invade the waters of these two rivers and their small tributary streams, while some of the less hardy contented themselves by staying on land, kicking up chunks of rocks and dirt or digging holes in the ground — and frequently being well rewarded.

Just as a swarm of bees must sooner or later come to rest on some spot and call it home, so these miners gradually settled down on a particular part of this ridge, largely because a squatter named William Dean had built a cabin there in the summer of 1832, shortly to be followed by Nathaniel Nuckolls, who more enterprisingly set up a small tavern. Around this convenience, a town would surely spring up, for back and sides might go bare but miners must have strong ale. Soon there was drawn together a population, described by one who was there, as "composed of all classes and conditions of the human family, from the most indigent beggar, to the wealthy nabob."[12] Or, according to another, a so-called poet, who was present and going under the new name of Billy:

> And as for people, they're so thick,
> That you might stir them with a stick;
> And every house you see will *grin*
> To show you what may be within.
> Of people, we've of every hue,
> Some white, red, yaller, *black and blue:*
> Others with dirt, so covered well,
> What color they, I could not tell.[13]

Such a place must certainly have a name and it was only natural for it first to be called Deans but shortly thereafter, more logically, Nuckollsville. This latter name seemed to have captured the popular imagination, for with the drunken miners frequently using their knuckles upon one another, it seemed a most appropriate one. The name Nuckollsville long continued to be used in jest. But as no settlement could ever grow into a respectable city under such a name, it became the task of the more scholarly part of the community to devise a better one.

It seems that no person was enterprising enough to offer a prize in a contest of name-choosing; but the honor of devising the name adopted was first mistakenly awarded to John C. Calhoun, who owned a mine in the vicinity and was much interested when he was here in the fall of 1832, in having an appropriate name chosen. A Doctor Croft of South Carolina, who had come along with Calhoun on this trip suggested the name Aureola, meaning *golden* or *shining like gold* and he would have the county, which had not yet been laid off and named Lumpkin, called Aldoradda, which was said to be a Spanish name, meaning *gold region*. These names suited Calhoun perfectly and so he called on the settlers to adopt them. The legislature a little later named the county Lumpkin, for Wilson Lumpkin, then governor of Georgia; and the people of the settlement named their place Auraria — not exactly the same name which Dr. Croft had selected but a name meaning about the same thing — that is *gold mine* or *gold region*. This name was selected by Major John Powell, a prominent citizen of the place,[14] and seemed to please everyone, including the enterprising editor of a newspaper, the *Western Herald,* which had been established here on April 9, 1833. According to the editor, the town's "locality justly entitles it to the name which it bears; being one as we conceive, of melodious sound, accompanied with classic taste, and appropriate derivation."[15] The poet Billy proved that he himself had a fertile mind for names:

If I say city, will that go?
For town nor borough will not do,
For this *bangs* all the borough race,
And is indeed "all sorts a'place."
Of given names it has its fill,
Once being Dean's, now Nuckollsville;
But some folks they begin to frown,
And call our city Scuffle-town;
When scholars comed with much array,
And christen'd it Auraria.
So I propose to end the ditty,
A purtier name for't *Chuckluck City*.[16]

But people in other parts of the state were somewhat puzzled by the name. The editor of the *Georgia Journal* guessed that as the town was in the cool mountains the name must come from the Latin word *aura,* meaning "a gentle gale of cool air";[17] but the editor of the Savannah *Georgian,* being either an accomplished Latin scholar or having a handy reference work nearby, knew better. He said Auraria was a Latin word which meant *gold mine* and that Tacitus had used it — and to satisfy those doubters who might ask him where, he cited "lib. 6. Cap. 19," adding that "the name of the town (Auraria) is as new to us as the town itself."[18]

So Auraria meant *gold mine,* and in that name lay the only reason why there was a town there at all. Rich man, poor man, beggar man, thief — all were there working like beavers, panning the streams and digging holes into the hills. Calhoun had come in early, and, as has been noted, he presided at the first attempt to christen Auraria. He and his associates were to be richly rewarded in working their nearby mine. Many who had been lucky drawers of gold lots in the lottery or who had quickly in a speculative venture bought lots from the lucky, were now offering them for sale.[19] In fact speculators expected to make as much money buying and selling gold lots as did those who worked them. In July 1833 one gold lot of forty acres was sold for $30,000.[20] Thomas Butler **King of Glynn County** was not selling lots at this particular time but he had secured with good titles twenty-seven lots, which he advertised by number and location and warned the public against purchasing them from speculators who might claim to own them.[21] Roswell King of Darien, down on the coast, had valuable mines around Auraria and to better protect his interests, he became a resident of Auraria.[22]

Colonel D. C. Gibson published to the world but especially "To Gold Mine Speculators" that he could be found at all times in Auraria or nearby and that for $25.00 he would test any lot in the gold region and would "warrant his opinion when given to be correct."[23] In early 1833 a man on the spot asserted that the mines were yielding "in rich abundance, the anticipated fruits of the most sanguine speculator,"[24] and six months later he supposed "on a moderate calculation, that 700,000 dollars worth of gold" had been "extracted from the mines in this county [Lumpkin], during the past season!" In booster fashion, he asked the rhetorical question, "What Cotton growing county in the state can compete with us."[25]

As scientific tests were later to show, Auraria ores produced a higher percentage of gold than did the California mines, later.[26] Five hands in one day's work panned out 160 pennyweight or 8 ounces of gold;[27] a resident of the neighborhood brought into town a nugget weighing 40 pennyweight; and Colonel Gibson, who was part owner of the Calhoun mine, brought in from that mine a chunk weighing nine pounds and three ounces "with one hundred and twenty-four particles of gold upon its surface, plainly perceptible to the eye."[28] But the greatest sensation was the discovery on Major Alfred B. Holt's lot near Auraria, of a rock weighing "between twenty and thirty pounds, with large particles of gold thickly interspersed in it, from the size of a pepper corn to that of a marble." It was one of the richest chunks ever seen. It was broken up and parts of it sent to Milledgeville and to New York, but the owner kept the "finest piece."[29]

A tin pan and a spade were all the equipment needed to work the branch deposits, on which Auraria first began to flourish;[30] but it was only a short time before more expensive equipment was being brought in. Soon two gold washing machines were up for sale;[31] and a little later licenses were being offered to use special "Patent Panning, Gold-washing Machines."[32] But more specifically, Colonel John Powell announced that he had applied for a patent on two types of gold washing machines which would supplant the rocking cradles then in use. Using the larger one, eight hands could wash in one hour three hundred bushels of grit "without losing any Gold." He warranted this machine "to wash more grit in a given time, than any five Machines now in use, and to lose less Gold than any one."[33] As the washing machines improved, they made it profitable to process the same gravel and grit a second and even a third time.[34] When it came to raising the sands and gravel out of the deep waters of the Chestatee and Etowah rivers, something more than pans and spades or even patented washing machines was needed. And now is when the diving bell made its appearance. A boat bearing such a contrivance was in early 1833 launched on the Chestatee River near Auraria,[35] creating a sensation, viewed by many including Billy the poet. And here is how Billy memorialized the occasion:

> Wend you to the Mines and see,
> The various things for your temptation,
> Stand on the banks of the Chestatee,
> Where the diving bell's in operation.
> Wend you to the pearly stream,
> Where your eyes must be delighted,
> Then of golden streets you'll dream,
> If perchance you get benighted.[36]

Gold in the sands of the Chestatee and of other streams was an indicator of great pockets from which these particles had escaped. The wise miner always hunts for the pockets, and within a year or two after the founding of Auraria when miners began to look for the pockets there arose vein mining high up on the ridges. This kind of mining made necessary

VALLEY OF THE CHESTATEE

the expenditure of money far beyond the capacity of the swarms of people who had come into Auraria. Before the end of 1833, an Aurarian said it was then high time for people to get away from the streams and accumulated deposits in the lowlands and get up into the highlands. Continuing, he said, "For the most of the deposit Mines must to a great extent exhaust in a few years, at the farthest. Then it will be that the miner's last hope will center upon the vein mines, the only thing in our opinion worthy of the name of a Gold mine."[37] Following his advice, the firm of Ware and Matthews by the summer of 1834 had sunk a mine 100 feet deep and had erected a small stamping mill.[38]

And it was not long before mining companies were being organized and were receiving charters from the state legislature. In December of 1834 the Pigeon-roost Mining Company was the first of the big capitalistic mining companies to be chartered. Allen Matthews and others, who owned four 40-acre gold lots "together with mills, machinery, and other property connected with the mining business," were incorporated under this name.[39] The next year the company offered to the public an issue of $400,000 in stock, and a booster thought that "Stock taken in it" would be "far more valuable than in any institution in the United States."[40] Chartered at the same time was another company under the name of the Belfast Mining Company, with an authorized capital stock of $500,000.[41]

Many prospectors who had been panning for themselves and who were becoming acquainted with the law of diminishing returns, now began to find employment with the big mining companies. In the autumn of 1833 a person terming himself an experienced miner with the best references, advertised in the local paper that he wished "to get employment in a mine, vein or deposit."[42] In fact a labor supply soon came to be one of the greatest concerns of the mining companies — laborers to do heavy work, such as only slaves could be induced to perform. Then news was soon abroad that "Strong Negro Men are in demand at the Mines, at $10 per month; and other hands in proportion."[43] A year later advertisements were running: "Liberal prices will be given for Negroes."[44] Large numbers of slaves were used in the mining operations, many of them being provided by planters in the cotton belt when times were slack there.

Mining was haphazard and wasteful and it was only for the reason that there was much gold around that the miners got anything worth while at all. A geologist and mining engineer traveling through the Auraria region in the 1850s wrote: "The amount of the gold distributed in the drift over the hills and valleys along the Chestatee and its tributaries is enormous, but cannot be calculated with precision. The evidences of its presence are on all sides as we pass over the roads or along the streams, but the fact that it is there in quantities is brought most forcibly to the mind in passing over the excavations made by the miners in the deposits since 1829. The beds of the creeks and brooks have been dug up, and the water now runs among unsightly heaps of gravel or through irregular pits."[45] Apart from luck on occasions, the early miners averaged hardly more than five to ten pennyweights a day.

Nobody knows or can know how much gold was taken from these Georgia mines, both in the rich Auraria and Lumpkin County region and in the rest of the state, for much of it found its way to market in channels apart from government mints and assay offices. But from 1828 through 1837 the Georgia gold which reached the Philadelphia mint amounted to $1,763,900. Practically all of this gold had been obtained from the streams and river flats.[46] The receipts at the Dahlonega mint in the first year of its establishment, 1838, amounted to $102,915. Down through the years as the gold production simmered off, Dahlonega received less and less until 1861 when the mint was closed, the receipts were only $60,946. During this whole period, the receipts at the Dahlonega mint amounted to $6,115,569. A careful estimate indicates that throughout the period of gold mining in Georgia down to 1896, something more than $16,000,000 was taken out of the ground.[47]

TRAVELING IN THE GOLD REGION

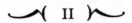
MERCHANTS, BANKERS, LAWYERS, BARBERS, DOCTORS, IN AURARIA

ABOUT everybody who came to Auraria was lured there by the glitter of gold, and as Billy the poet said,

> I spose you'se often times been told,
> That this here country's made o' gold.

And he continued his informative doggerel:

> But then agin, we've clever fellows,
> As Doctors, Lawyers, and Gold sellers;
> The Doctors *scace*, the Lawyers plenty,
> I reckon we have nearly twenty.
> And Merchants too to save each penny,
> I could not count them, they're so many.[1]

But all who came did not expect to dig their gold out of the ground. It was easier to get it from the miner who had got it by digging; this had been so, long before Auraria ever grew up and it would remain true long thereafter. Most miners had always dug their gold not to keep but to spend and all mining towns before, now, and henceforth, had made, were making, and would make it easy for them to do so. There were many things that the miners must have and there were many other things which they wanted merely for pleasure.

Auraria soon got ready to satisfy the wants of all. An

Aurarian before the town was a year old noted that its growth was "unprecedented in any back country village in the southern States." Here on this 40-acre gold lot there were one hundred dwelling houses, "eighteen or twenty stores; twelve or fifteen law offices; and four or five Taverns, &c." Its population was estimated at 1,000 and it was thought that 10,000 people were living in the county, and in both town and county "constantly increasing, with a rapidity almost too incredible to relate." Practically all these people were white (or colored slaves), for most of the Indians who had once been here left after they had relinquished their rights to the soil.[2]

Probably the first institution which seemed most needful to the visitor arriving in Auraria was a tavern. The presence of such an institution had been responsible for Auraria springing up on lot 664, district 12, of section 1, instead of on some other lot.[3] Though Nathaniel Nuckolls had set up the first tavern, his was not first in the point of respectability, sentiment, or longevity. This honor went to Mrs. George W. Paschal, Grandma Paschal as she came affectionately to be called. She was the widow of a Revolutionary soldier, who with a family of children, sons and daughters, had moved to Auraria during the first year of the town's existence. She came from Lexington, Oglethorpe County, where she had previously run a tavern.[4] "Mrs. Paschal & Sons" soon announced that they had opened a "house of entertainment" which had previously been "occupied by Mr. Nuckolls," who had "resigned his entire business to their care." They promised their guests "as good accommodations as the country" afforded.[5] A few months later the Paschals moved into a "new Framed Building" in the north end of town, where they were prepared "to entertain in a comfortable manner" all persons who might give them a call.[6] Mrs. Paschal, being a religious and moral woman, allowed no strong drinks to be served in her establishment.

For many residents of a gold-mining town and for visitors

too, a tavern without a bar was unthinkable. It were better
that it have no roof. A desire by people with gold need only
to be known in order to be catered to. R. A. Watkins soon
secured possession of the old Paschal house and after giving
it a thorough repairing, he named it Miners Hall, and announced that his table would be provided with the best food
that could be found. His stables under the direction of an
"attentive ostler" would supply plenty of provender, and his
bar would serve "the best of liquors."[7] William Rogers ran
a tavern on Main Street, honoring the Indians by naming it
the Cherokee Hotel and catering especially to the traveler
looking for information on the gold-mining regions.[8] Also
Thomas Westbrook opened "a house of entertainment," and
he announced: "His tables will be furnished with the best the
country affords, his bar supplied with choice liquors, his
stables with plenty of provender, and no exertions spared
. . . conducive to the comfort and convenience of the traveller." He promised that his charges would be "as moderate
as the hardness of times will admit of."[9]

Those making their way to Auraria but getting caught by
darkness on the Chestatee River, at Leather's Ford, four
miles away, were invited by William Ragan to stop at the
Traveler's Home. He promised a commodious establishment
with suitable rooms for families or private persons, a table
with good food, stables "with plenty of provender," and a bar
with "choice Liquors."[10]

If Auraria had a thousand people and the county, ten
thousand, then there were outstanding business opportunities
here, for no other towns had yet grown up in this region. It
might well be expected that Major Powell, who had chosen
the name Auraria, would develop various financial and business interests in the place. And so it was. Under the firm
name of John M. Powell & Company he ran one of those
"eighteen or twenty stores." He had a general assortment of
groceries which he offered at wholesale or retail "at very low
prices for Cash only." Soon he was offering bargains because

he had decided to go out of the grocery business.[11] A. M'Laughlin & Company had $4,000 worth of merchandise, consisting mostly of dry goods and groceries which they were selling extremely cheap. It seems that this firm was primarily interested in the wholesale business, supplying other merchants, as it announced that persons "wishing to embark in the business in the Gold Region, and in a populus and flourishing Village" would do well "to call without delay at the Store, and examine for themselves."[12]

S. T. Rowland's establishment came nearest to qualifying as a great department store of a later age. In listing at great length what he had for sale he gave future generations an insight into what a person living on the frontiers of the Georgia gold-mining region might enjoy if he had the "Cash or Gold" with which to pay for it; for Rowland was selling at low prices for "Cash or Gold" only. He announced that he had recently received from New York and Charleston "a well selected assortment of Dry-Goods, Groceries, Hardware & Crockery" and then he specified more particularly. He had 4,000 yards of "Sheeting and Shirting" and 2,000 yards of "Cheap Negro Cloth." Some of the other articles he had for sale were: "London Duffle Blankets," "Cotton Diapers," calico, "Turkey Red Prints," ginghams, bombazetts, shawls, Irish linen, "Satinett, Silk & Cotton Flag" handkerchiefs, ready-made clothing, molasses, St. Croix sugar, New Orleans and New England rum, coffee, Holland gin, cognac, peach brandy, Madeira wine, champagne, claret, port, muscat, malaga, London porter, soap, rice, 5,000 "Spanish Segars," crackers, mackerel, sperm candles, almonds, herring, tobacco, raisins, spades, shovels, blacksmith tools, saws, nails, window glass, knives and forks, "Pocket, Pen and Dirk Knives," razors, scissors, shears, locks, rifles, shot guns, "Everpointed Pencils," pens, carpenter tools, china and glass ware, axes, tea kettles, tinware, and wool and fur hats. He was in the market for gold and would give the highest price for it.[13]

H. C. & G. C. Bradford's announcement of articles kept in

stock included about all which Rowland had and they offered additionally "Blue, Black and Invisible Cloths," "Shoes and Boots," and such hardware as "Chissels, Augers, Handsaws and Hammers, Hinges, Waffle Irons, Grid Irons, Pad Locks," and "Knives and Razors, Spades and Shovels." This firm's goods came from Baltimore and Philadelphia.[14] John H. Ware decided to specialize in only one branch of the mercantile business. He ran a confectionery and promised to keep in stock everything which anyone should expect in such a store. But he issued this warning: "You who call must not expect to find me in a fine Building, still you will find the best of articles, at my old prices, *for Cash only.*"[15]

In Auraria as in any other booming frontier mining town, heretofore or hereafter, where ranching had not yet penetrated or agriculture made a lodgment, prices might be expected to be high and nothing but "cash or Gold" acceptable. In addition to high prices there was scarcity in certain articles. In the summer of 1834 there was little bacon in Lumpkin County and not a pound for sale.[16] The following prices were current in the early spring of the preceding year, published with the comment that the articles listed were "in much demand in this market," and with this additional explanation of the situation around Auraria: "The infancy of the country, and the consequent scarcity of provisions, affords [*sic*] inducements to the agriculturalists of the adjacent counties, to look to this as a market for their surplus produce."

> *Corn*—75 to 87½ cents per bushel
> *Meal*—87½ cents to $1.00 per bushel
> *Fodder*—$2.50 to $3.00 per hundred pounds
> *Flour*—$10.00 per barrel
> *Butter*—18¾ to 25 cents per pound
> *Chickens*—12½ to 18¾ cents per pound
> *Vegetables*—"In proportion"
> *Board*—$12.00 to $15.00 per month for man
> *Horse*—$10.00 to $12.00 per month.[17]

Six months later prices were about the same, with these additional items quoted: *Eggs*—12½ to 18¾ cents per dozen; *Potatoes*—50 to 75 cents per bushel; *Turnips*— 25 to 37½ cents per bushel. Of typical mountain products, *Chestnuts* were quoted as "Scarce" and *Chinquapins,* "None on the market,"[18] and surprisingly two other mountain products, bear meat and venison, were not even mentioned. But a good reason may have been that all human denizens of the mountains were too busy looking for gold nuggets to be lured into hunting bears and deer.

It should be noted that in all market quotations in the Aurarian region, bacon was never included in the lists, even to note its scarcity. Yet the supply of bacon was not always short, nor, of turkeys; for that spectacular and almost unbelievable device of getting livestock and fowls to market, quite common in the Southern Highlands during the first third of the nineteenth century, was carried on to and through Auraria. This was the hog drives, cattle drives, and turkey drives. There were even duck drives, but none appears to have come through the Auraria country. These drives originated generally in East and Middle Tennessee, but sometimes as far away as Kentucky. They followed the river valleys and gorges through the mountains and across the ridges at the low gaps; and the drovers, whether driving hogs, cattle, turkeys, or ducks, sometimes continued on as far as Charleston or Savannah — though they were more likely to sell out in Spartanburg or Augusta, with Auraria and other smaller towns on the way having aided the drovers in reducing their charges. The hog drovers had their own doggerel verses and folk songs attuned to the business they were engaged in, as

> Hog drovers, hog drovers, hog drovers we air,
> A-courting your darter, so purty and fair.

The turkey drovers had to be more on the alert than the hog drovers, for though the hogs were stubborn and head-

strong and generally tried to go in the direction opposite to
that in which they were being prodded, the turkeys while
more amenable to the urgings of the drover during daylight,
when eventide came on, paid no attention to the drover as
they took to the trees, following that instinct as old as the
tribe of turkeys themselves. Turkey drovers, therefore, tried
to time their day's travel to reach certain fixed stations by
nightfall. Also, turkey drovers had to be up early in the
morning to gather together their flock to keep it from spreading throughout the woods as it flew down from its perches.
There was a special "turkey station" near Auraria which the
turkey drovers tried to reach before nightfall. The hog
drovers also found accommodations on the outskirts of the
town, where slaughter pens had been erected to take care of
the hogs the Aurarians should buy.[19]

If business were to be carried on profitably and expedi-
tiously, there must be a medium of exchange circulating in a
sufficient amount to take care of that business and a medium
having a value not given to rapid fluctuation. In Auraria no
one was willing to sell on credit — sales must be for "cash or
Gold." As there was a great deal more gold in this region
than there was cash, the first financial worry to develop was
how to measure gold and market it and at what price — for
after all raw gold was as much a commodity on the market
as was bread and meat. And buying something in exchange
for gold was in reality only barter. Just as merchants advertised articles for sale, they announced that not only would
they accept gold in payment, but also they would buy gold
without reference to receiving it in exchange for goods. As
merchant S. T. Rowland put it: "Highest price given for
Gold."[20] Banks in the southeastern United States had their
agents in Auraria bidding for gold, and even Samuel J. Bee-
bee, "Stock and Exchange Broker, 21 Wall Street, New-
York," advertised in the Auraria newspaper that at all times
he would give for gold the highest price.[21]

In April 1833, the price of gold on the Aurarian market

was from 85 to 92 cents per pennyweight, "according to its
fineness." It was reported that gold "collected in this neighborhood will average 90 cents, when well cleansed, when
fluxed and run into bars, 92 cents."[22] A miner who came to
town with his gold in the form in which he had found it, in
grains and nuggets, was at a great disadvantage in using it in
that shape as a medium of exchange, and the merchant who
might receive it was equally so. The scales might be depended on for correct weight, but what was the fineness of
the gold? Nothing but a gold laboratory could answer this
question, and that experienced gold miner Major John
Powell was the man to come to the rescue. Soon he announced that he and John N. Rose had set up a laboratory
"for the purpose of Assaying, Refining, and Fluxing GOLD,
and analysing every description of metallic ore." All miners
and purchasers of gold were promised that these operations
would be "conducted with care and accuracy."[23]

Gold bars correctly weighed and stamped served very well
as money, except that not necessarily being of uniform
weight they could not be used handily in many transactions
where change had to be given. To get around this difficulty
certain people trained in purifying, fluxing, and assaying
gold issued coins under their own names, in no wise coun-
terfeiting United States coins, but as true to the value
stamped on them and circulating as readily as United States
coins. Two well-known private coiners in the southeastern
United States were Christopher Bechtler and Templeton
Reid, the one in the North Carolina gold regions and the
other in the Aurarian country. Reid's coins were actually
worth more than their face value, and counterfeiters, therefore, found it more advantageous to copy Reid's money
rather than that of the United States.[24] It was not considered
illegal for a private minter to issue coins of his own design,
stamped with his name and the value, for although the
Federal Constitution gave Congress the right to coin money
and regulate its value, and denied this right to the states, it

was not an exclusive right and did not operate against individuals. As a New York editor commented at the time,
Reid was doubtless "of the Virginia school of strict construction," who not being a state found "himself at liberty to
exercise this high attribute of sovereignty."[25]

Reid set up his mint at Gainesville, and was issuing coins
there in 1830, immediately after gold had been discovered in
the Cherokee country and two years before Auraria, about
fifteen miles to the northwest, sprang up. He issued $2.50,
$5.00, and $10.00 pieces and coined about $700.00 a day. As
his profits were estimated at about 7 per cent, his yearly
income was about $15,000.00. "This is better business than
gold digging," remarked the *Charleston Courier*.[26] Yet of
the many coins he issued, a century later only six $5.00 pieces
were known to be in existence, one of which was sold for
$1,325.[27]

It was a tribute to the miners' respect for governmental
institutions, that irrespective of how good Templeton Reid's
coins were (and they did not know at that time how high
they were to rate), they would not rest content until they
could get a United States assay office and mint in their very
midst, and thus be relieved of sending their gold to the far-
away Philadelphia Mint. And even if Templeton Reid's
coins were worth more than their face value, that was only
part of the story, for what assurances had the miners that
Reid would pay as high a price for gold as could be got at
a United States mint? When a miner sold his gold to the
trade he had to accept some sort of money in exchange for
it, and what he generally got were the notes "of rotten
Banks." With a mint, an Aurarian remarked, "We shall be
enabled to get for the stuff in its native unwrought state the
real Jackson shiners themselves."[28] This was not purely a
miners' problem, it had to do with all business transactions
wherein money was used. By 1833 there had begun to circulate "an immense number of Dimes or ten cent pieces,"
which were "passed off or put upon the people, at twenty

five per Cent above their real value," to the great injury of
the people. Various merchants and trades people made public announcement that they would not accept more than one
dime in any transaction, at more than its face value.[29]

The movement to induce Congress to establish a mint in
Georgia got started as early as 1830. During the next few
years it gained momentum. Soon a meeting in Auraria organized a campaign, having readily enlisted the support of
John C. Calhoun, who owned a gold mine nearby. With
Thomas Hart Benton ("Old Bullion") and Calhoun supporting a mint, Congress passed a law establishing one five miles
north of Auraria, at Dahlonega, a recently-come rival town.
The mint was completed in 1837 and began operating the
next year.[30] It continued until 1861 when it was seized by
Georgia on the outbreak of the Civil War. It was never re-
established.

The mint was to have its place in the monetary needs of
the Aurarian country, but it could not solve all of the problems; and as noted, it was some years before the mint was
established. In the meantime the Aurarians were calling
loudly for banking facilities, and some of the Georgia banks
were beginning to discover opportunities for themselves in
the gold region just as were lawyers, merchants, and doctors.
The first move toward establishing a bank in Auraria was
made at a meeting on November 12, 1833, at the tavern
which was run by Mrs. Paschal & Sons. At this preliminary
meeting it was decided to appoint a committee of eight to
inquire into the expediency of approaching the legislature
to charter such an institution. Four days later another meeting was called at the same tavern, at which the committee
made its report. It noted that "almost the entire currency
of this section of the state is of Bank Notes, issued from
Banks of this State located at a great distance." As most of
the supplies in the Aurarian country came from upper Georgia and the nearby parts of Tennessee, North Carolina, and
South Carolina, and had to be paid for in bank notes from

a region with which Aurarians and their creditors had no commercial transactions, these notes did not circulate here at par, but at a discount ranging from 3 to 5 per cent. If Auraria had a bank and should issue notes, backed by gold as they would be, they would circulate at par, and Auraria would thus be relieved of this loss. The committee recommended that "such of our citizens who are able to concentrate a capital, . . . form a company among themselves, for the purpose of buying gold under proper rules and restrictions, . . . and that when a company sufficiently strong can be established, that they petition the Legislature to incorporate them as a body politic, with power to emit bills payable at home, for whatever amount of gold may be received." This report was unanimously agreed to.[31]

Before such a bank could be organized, the Pigeon-roost Mining Company, which had secured a charter in December, 1834, began certain financial operations in connection with its mining activities, that smacked much of banking, though it had not been given banking privileges. It issued an attractive note, in all appearances a bank note, at the top right of which the Goddess of Plenty was shaking gold coins from a cornucopia and at the left stood a Cherokee Indian with drawn bow and arrow; but the note did not presumably have the privilege of circulating as money except as the individual owner might induce its receipt, for it was made out to a person by name and was an order on the treasurer of the Mining Company. Very likely these notes did circulate in the vicinity before some holder presented them to the Company for payment.[32] But this Pigeon-roost Mining Company was not a bank and it did not serve the needs Aurarians had for a bank.

The Aurarians themselves never got to the point of establishing their contemplated bank, for the Bank of Darien, which had various branches scattered over Georgia, decided to add another branch at Auraria. It already had an agent in Auraria for the purpose of buying gold and sending it out, but this activity was far short of what a bank would do. However, it was not this fact alone which induced the Darien bank to extend its activities to Auraria. Early in 1834 Thomas C. Bowen, a native Irishman, was intrusted by the Aurarian agent of the Darien Bank, with 14,950 penny-weights of gold to be taken to Savannah. This amount of gold outweighed Bowen's sense of honesty; instead of taking it to Savannah, he disappeared with it. A letter from him, postmarked in Charleston, explained that "he could not withstand the temptation, that pursuit would be useless, and that his creditors might make the best of his goods he had left behind."[33]

Even before the Bowen episode, it had been reported that the Bank of Darien had "determined to establish a Branch in Auraria,"[34] and now there was every reason to hurry up the move. So in the year 1834 Auraria could boast of a bank. Almost forty years later, George W. Paschal remembered that "Thomas King" was "president or cashier of a small bank in Auraria."[35] Paschal was here confusing Thomas Butler King with Roswell King. Roswell King was the cashier and a member of the board of directors.[36]

It should hardly be expected that there would be any manufacturing establishments in a frontier settlement like Auraria, but A. Johnson published the fact that he was erecting a tin factory and would soon be making and keeping on hand all sorts of tinware, which he would sell wholesale or retail, but, like all the other careful businessmen of this time and place, for cash only.[37]

A tailor and a tinsmith might not have belonged to the same guild in the Middle Ages, but both fashioned raw or semi-raw materials into something which could be used more advantageously. Auraria could boast of only one tinsmith but it had several tailors, all keenly competing for the business of clothing the male population of Auraria. There was J. J. Land, who declared that "if strict attention to business, and good work" would gain him "the patronage of the pub-

lic," he was "determined to have it."[38] Also there was the
firm of D. A. Wiles and W. S. Sanders, who gave "every
pledge on their part to please the fancy and tastefully fit all
those who patronize them in their business." They received
the latest New York and Philadelphia fashions.[39] Partner
Wiles of this firm and late of Athens, Tennessee, seemed to
run a tailoring business also under his own name, for he
announced that he received monthly "New-York, Philadelphia, and Baltimore fashions" and hoped "from assiduous
attention to business to merit a share of public patronage."[40]
And B. C. Candee, another tailor, flattered "himself, from
his experience in business" that he would be able "to give
general satisfaction" and he warranted all work done "to be
equal to that done in Augusta, or elsewhere." He added:
"Work done according to the most approved fashion or to
order."[41]

Barbers had nothing to sell except their services. Auraria
had one who advertised himself "Alexander Scott, Barber
and Hair Dresser," and who told about his work in the most
approved doggerel of his times. He

> Informs the friends who on him call,
> That he's prepared to shave them all;
> His razors now are very keen,
> The stiffest beard to shave quite clean.
> Soaps, Oils, and Towels, the senses greet,
> They look so fair, and smell so sweet.
> His scissors too, make dandies smile,
> They cut the hair in such fine style.
> And Travellers who may visit here,
> Would prosper under Alex's care;
> For 'tis his great and chief delight,
> To make rough faces, a comely sight.
> For all past favors, he now sends,
> His grateful thanks to all his friends;
> And tho' in Latin he's no sponsor,
> Yet signs himself their humble
>
> TONSOR.[42]

Barbers and tailors might not have rated the high appellation of professional men, but doctors and lawyers, who at that time went through little more preparatory study, would likely have been highly incensed not to have been so classified. A settlement with as many people as Auraria had could hardly have got along without physicians, and physicians could hardly have stayed away from such a place which had so much gold in it — even though Aurarians were frequently denying to the rest of the world that there was any sickness there, and bragging that it was one of the healthiest spots in the nation. It might be said that doctors of medicine literally presided at the birth of Auraria and saw it into the world. Foremost in point of time there — or at least .the first to let himself be known in print as having located there — was Dr. Ira A. Foster, who promised to "attend to calls in the various branches of his profession."[43] Before Auraria was a year old Dr. John H. Thomas from Middle Georgia announced his presence in Auraria, making the promise of "charges in proportion with the times, and strict attention to calls" and expressing the hope that he might "merit a share of public patronage."[44] And soon Dr. J. D. Rivers had come,[45] later to be followed by others.

Lawyers, who in the early days had been excluded from Georgia, sensed from afar that there was business in Auraria, that this region was as rich in disputes and lawsuits as it was in gold nuggets. In addition to the ordinary grist that went into the lawyer's mill were the disputes over the ownership of gold lots, speculators selling lots which did not belong to them, squatters settling wherever they pleased, and intruders digging on lands which they did not own.[46] Among the first lawyers to arrive in Auraria was George W. Paschal. The Paschal family down in Oglethorpe County, now in low circumstances, had enjoyed for a time high hopes that out of the eleven draws the various members of the family had a right to exercise in the gold lottery, they might be lucky enough to win at least one lot. In January 1833, before the

lottery had been concluded, Paschal went up to Auraria to
spy out the possibilities there for a representative of his profession. Prospects appearing good, he returned to his old
home and brought back his mother (Grandma Paschal) and
the rest of the family.[47] Though he was listed as one of the
tavern firm of "Mrs. Paschal & Sons," his chief business was
practicing law, with his office in the tavern.[48]

Among those "twelve or fifteen law offices" in Auraria in
early 1833, was that of William E. Walker, who announced
that he was ready "to attend to the collection of executions
against fortunate drawers; and to the prosecution and defending of cases of fraudulent draws; and all other business
connected with his profession. . . ."[49] Also there were Isaac
R. Walker, who promised to attend to business throughout
the Cherokee Circuit and the adjoining counties of the Western Circuit;[50] the firm of Alfred B. Holt & Hines Holt, who
announced the same extended practice and added the adjoining counties of the Chattahoochee Circuit;[51] J. J. Hutchinson,
who was "prepared to attend to any business in his professional line which may be confided to him";[52] Ezekiel W.
Cullers, who would "thankfully receive and promptly attend
to . . . all business entrusted to his care";[53] Milton H. Gathright, always ready for business;[54] Allen Matthews, whose
office was in "the north end of town";[55] and Stephen Douglas
Crane, who in addition to being a lawyer, had had the experience of three years in gold mining and " (assisted by Mr.
George S. Moody, from North Carolina)" he would "act as
agent in the examination, and sale of gold lots."[56]

Some lawyers over the state who wanted to help enjoy a
part of the prosperity of Auraria but who were already settled
in lucrative practice in their own towns, entered into copart-
nerships with Auraria lawyers. Edward Harden, a prominent
lawyer in Athens, toyed with the idea of moving into the
Cherokee Circuit, " (perhaps *Auraria*, Lumpkin County)"
but he compromised with his ambition by forming a partnership with James Rogers, already at Auraria. Rogers was to

look after the Aurarian end and Harden to remain in Athens and look after affairs from that end.[57] Similarly the law firm of William H. Underwood and Allen G. Fambrough was formed, with Underwood continuing his office in Gainesville and Fambrough setting one up in Auraria.[58]

Auraria had a further attraction for lawyers during its first year, for it was the county seat and was frequently referred to as Lumpkin Court House and given that mailing address. Here the Superior Court judge attended to the business that came to him in Lumpkin County. In late June 1833 Judge John W. Hooper held hearings in chambers here for two days, being concerned mostly with bills of injunction; but to take part in the proceedings, a galaxy of lawyers assembled themselves, some already well-known and others to gain renown, some from Auraria and others from out of town. "Long and powerful speeches" made the little log courthouse room ring with oratory. There was Eli S. Shorter, a prominent lawyer from Columbus; William H. Underwood, long to be important in the state's legal history; Garnett Andrews, a famous wit, a judge later of the Northern Circuit, and in his old age the author of the Georgia classic *Reminiscences of an Old Georgia Lawyer;* and Thomas Jefferson Rusk, born in South Carolina, now living in the adjoining county of Habersham, and two years later to go to Texas and play an outstanding part in setting up the Republic of Texas, and dying in 1857 as United States Senator from Texas.[59]

Auraria was a strategic location and a veritable heaven for lawyers, not only because it was the seat of justice for Lumpkin County but also because the town itself soon developed a cluster of lawsuits. The land on which the town grew up belonged to the state of Georgia when the first settlers came in, and not until February 7, 1833 was this particular 40-acre gold lot drawn in the gold lottery and thereby became private property. The settlers, who had been squatters up to this time, now were transformed into trespassers. Remarkably enough this lot was drawn by a family of orphans, the children of Jesse Champion, who lived down in Newton County.[60]

In early April the guardian of the orphans came to Auraria and made temporary arrangements with the people, but the Aurarians sooner or later had to be brought to the final goal of buying the lots which they occupied either for residences or for business establishments. Otherwise they would have to pay rent, leave, or be brought before a court of justice. In the late summer of 1833, the guardian of the orphans, whose name was William K. Briers, advertised that this land would be sold "at public outcry" the following November. It would be divided into lots varying in size from 60 feet by 105 feet to 515 feet by 615 feet. Hoping, of course, to boost the price to be obtained for lots by giving a glowing picture of the location, Briers described Auraria as a thriving town on a ridge between the waters of two rivers, "and as regards salubrity of air, purity of water, fertility of soil, and quantity of the most precious metal" it was "surpassed by no neighborhood in the Southern States." In the "rapidity of improvement," it was "unequalled by any town or village in Georgia; and, as the sources of its prosperity" were "inexhaustible, its importance must be durable."[61] On the appointed day the lots were sold, but for only $2,089. This was considered a good price, however, for people were a little skeptical of Auraria's future, because the seat of justice had recently been moved to another place.[62] Apparently some purchasers did not complete their transactions but chose to become renters. In January of the next year the guardian of the orphans was threatening to sue all who had not paid their rent by the 10th of February.[63]

⊸(III)⊶

EDITOR, PREACHERS,
SCHOOLMASTERS

A TOWN of Auraria's size and promise could hardly be expected to get along without a newspaper, and certainly as long as there were enterprising editors in the land, one would soon discover the opportunities at Auraria. Such a person was shortly in the field, publishing his prospectus and raising subscriptions for a newspaper to be called the *Herald of the Gold Region,* and it should not be surprising that he lived in Athens; for the gold fever was strong in this piedmont Georgia town and had already propelled to the gold country several of its lawyers and speculators. Albon Chase was this newspaper prospector, who having drawn into this venture an unnamed partner, had issued his prospectus under the name of Albon Chase & Co. Chase was at this time the proprietor of the Athens *Southern Banner* and was in editorial partnership with Alfred M. Nisbet. He had purchased from O. P. Shaw in March 1832 an Athens newspaper called the *Athenian,* and changing its name to the *Southern Banner,* had brought out the first issue on March 20th following.

According to the prospectus, the *Herald of the Gold Region* was to be a weekly and be "published at Lumpkin Court House," a name still being used for Auraria. Stating the need for such a paper, Chase explained that the "recent or-

The Western Herald.

It comes, the Herald of a Golden World.

VOL. I.   AURARIA, LUMPKIN COUNTY, APRIL 23, 1833.   NO. 3.

PUBLISHED EVERY TUESDAY MORNING
BY O. P. SHAW,
AND
Edited by A. G. FAMBROUGH.

POETRY.

THIS WORLD AND THE NEXT.

SPEECH
OF
MR. FOSTER, OF GEORGIA,
On the Bill further to provide for the Collection
of the duties on imports.

ganization, and the rapid settlement and improvements now going on in that interesting portion of the territory of Georgia, known as the Cherokee Country, seem to require that an additional vehicle of public intelligence should be added to the number already located in different parts of our State. For that purpose is this harbinger of the forthcoming 'Herald' presented." He explained further that its "location in by far the richest part of the Gold Region, and where nature has signally blended the romantic with the sublime" would "give it advantages for the accomplishment of these objects, to which but few" could lay claim. He set March 19, 1833 as the day for the publication of the first issue.[1]

But before that day arrived, Chase decided that it might not be wise to attempt to run two newspapers in towns as far apart as Athens and Auraria, and so by mutual agreement with his partner, who was most likely O. P. Shaw, he gave up the venture. Whether Shaw had been Chase's partner or not, there appeared on the streets of Auraria, April 9, 1833 a newspaper called the *Western Herald,* with this motto, "It comes, the Herald of a Golden World." It was published by O. P. Shaw with Allen G. Fambrough as editor, a lawyer-resident of Auraria but recently from Gainesville. Fambrough remained the editor until January 11, 1834, when he was succeeded by J. J. Hutchinson, another resident lawyer. Shaw, the proprietor, continued to reside in Athens, though it may well be inferred that he visited Auraria frequently.[2]

The *Western Herald* was published on Tuesday mornings and it continued to appear on that day of the week until August 10th, when it changed to Saturday morning. Regularly thereafter as long as the paper lasted, it appeared on Saturday morning, excepting December 7, when it did not appear at all for that week.

For skipping a number, the editor gave this explanation: "The change in our weather gave us solemn warning to leave our transparent abode, and seek some other, more congenial to our *devil's fingers* and feelings, than the one we then occupied. The whistling of the westlin winds and northern blasts, as they played their Aeolian strains through the varied dimensions of our Lumpkin *star-lights,* might suit very well fiery fancy of a poet, or the musical ear of a minstrel, but they are too refrigerating for the geniuses of our *devils,* whose musical fingers must be kept at a proper temperature. The removal then of our office to a house more suitable for the approaching winter, engrossed so much of our time, that we were compelled to postpone the publication of last week's paper."[3] To recruit prospects out of whom the editor expected to develop printing devils, he now and then inserted notices in his paper such as this one: "Wanted at this Office two smart lads as apprentices to the printing business."[4]

Editor Fambrough gave this as a sufficient explanation for starting his newspaper: "The recent settlement and rapid improvement of this highly interesting section of Georgia, is deemed a sufficient apology in the estimation of the Proprietor and Editor of this paper, for establishing an additional source of intelligence to the one already in operation,[5] in that part of the State, known as the Cherokee country." Although he could not hope to satisfy the "wants and inclinations of the great mass of those, who may from time to time, look to this harbinger, for pleasing intelligence of the passing times," still he intended "to convey the usual newspaper intelligence, together with such other information in relation to the mining operations in this, and the surrounding country, as the Editor may be able to gather from sources that can be relied on, and such literary original essays as his time and talent may enable him to furnish." In politics the paper promised "the advancement of the doctrines inculcated in the Jeffersonian school, and cherished in Georgia in 1825, by what was then known here as the Troup party."[6]

The paper was dignified in format, neatly printed, and served well Auraria and the Cherokee country. The printing office was furnished with "a great variety of Type," and the editor promised to do job work "of every description, in a style" which it was hoped would "be perfectly satisfactory to applicants."[7] Soon the office announced that it had material on hand enabling it to print "fancy Bordering, Coloured Cards,"[8] suitable, no doubt, for birthday and Christmas greetings — and probably for Valentine Day, too.

The *Western Herald* received a welcome among the editors of the state and some of its editorials were widely copied.[9] It lived up to its promise to give to those interested the news of the mining country and to give to the mining country the news of the state and nation, including now and then a humorous allusion to Davy Crockett who was then as interested in exploiting himself in that vein for political advancement as a century and more later others were to exploit him for a different reason.[10] Apart from Fambrough's editorials there was not much that could be classified as "literary original essays," except the antics in doggerel of Billy the poet and of those who aided and abetted him —

> All hail! to the Bard — let the Gold diggers know it,
> Billy my Cousin, is the Nuckollsville poet![11]

And now and then there was a bit of unrhyming verse from "Tibicen Monteum," such as his lugubrious "Day Dreams," of which four lines were

> O! could I recall those days,
> Again dream o'er my hopeful story;
> Shake off life's dark realities,
> And light the waste of memory.[12]

A clever prose writer sent in an original contribution "prescribing a few rules by which to conduct, what is usually termed a *courtship*," in which he suggested the lack of wisdom in a lovelorn young swain who might express his feelings toward the young lady of his affection in a letter to her; for in such a letter "more is pledged than is ever performed, and consequently more is preserved than was ever true." Signing himself "Juvenis," he offered in derision this kind of poetry which the young lady would likely write back:

> These lines to you my friend,
> Will surely make an end
> Of what you mostly wish to hear,
> And sure you need not fear,
> That I'll for another care,
> No, I am your's, and you are mine,
> And till we wed Oh! haste the time.[13]

But in particular, the original literary efforts published in the *Western Herald* centered more around politics and the political issues of the times, and in this realm appeared contributions by such pen-name writers as "Powhatan," "One of the Old Troup Party," "Dr. Sell State," "Col. Tom Trott," "Hal Lightfoot," and "Westward Ho."

The press, the church, the school — all were necessary in the moral advancement of a people crowded together, and especially in a mining town such as Auraria. Here it should be easiest for a newspaper to make its way, for even among a rough population the pen could be made mightier than the sword, and even the sword could be brought to the support of the pen when belligerent editors challenged their enemies to duels. But no Aurarian editor was ever forced to such extremity.

Just as some of the early Kentucky frontiersmen proudly boasted that they had not brought Sunday across the mountains, so Aurarians might well have boasted that they had not brought a preacher into the Cherokee country. And as Billy, the "Nuckollsville poet," observed,

> You'll hear the noise as I was saying,
> But are not pestered with the praying.[14]

And just as a Kentucky bully could boast that he was a snapping turtle and could whip his weight in wildcats, according to the Nuckollsville poet one Aurarian swore that "it was his natur" to be "A real snapping Alligatur."[15] Long years after Auraria had been founded, a tradition grew up that there was not a rock in the place which had not at some time been banged against someone's head.

But before Auraria was a year old, evil reports were being spread of the wickedness which prevailed there. In answer to one such slander, the editor of the *Western Herald* replied: "We have here a population, the number of which, would reflect great credit to a city which had not been settled longer than this place, and this number too, has been collected from all parts of the Union, and placed here without any sort of municipal regulation; with no shackles of restraint around them, except their consciences, and the laws of the country, and we defy the world with such a number, brought together under such circumstances, to produce a precedent for good order and respectability among those that we consider citizens of the place." "It is true," he continued, "that many people visit here . . . , whose moral example, has neither been felt, seen, nor heard of among us, for the best of reasons, because they have not 'let their light shine' unless it was in dissipation, during their stay here; and then go off and lay the whole of it on the citizens of the place. It is true, that visitors seem to view this as the most favorable spot of all others for them to take their sprees and amusements; and the reason is very plain, for when they meet here, all strangers together, they are so completely masked, as to be beyond the fear of detection, and there are many who come here, just to go in for a frolic. But it is that sort of conduct that can injure none except, they engage in it; for we hear of no midnight assassins; no pocket picking; no robberies; no stealing of any kind. . . ." The calumniator "must have kept the very worst company that resorts to the place, and then he must not only have exaggerated greatly, but lied most egregiously. . . ." The editor assured "the public, that we have good Taverns here, kept by responsible men, and a population able, and at all times willing to protect the persons and property of individuals who visit this place, who conduct themselves in a decent, and becoming manner."[16]

Although those who settled Auraria brought no preacher

with them, there came during the first year Agnes Paschal,
the widow of the Revolutionary soldier George W. Paschal,
the mother of George W. Paschal (Jr.), the lawyer — "Grandma Paschal, the Angel of Auraria." No liquors flowed in her
tavern with the good food she served. She was determined
to develop a moral atmosphere in Auraria by promoting
religion and by becoming a Florence Nightingale many years
before that name came to have humanitarian significance.
Whenever there was sickness or want Grandma Paschal was
on hand, however dark or stormy the night might be.

Grandma Paschal had scarcely arrived in Auraria before
she set out to organize a Baptist church, sending one of her
sons with a subscription list through the town. Soon she had
collected enough money to build a rude log church and clear
away a plot for a graveyard — for she was determined that
her husband in his lonely grave at the old dilapidated home-
stead near Lexington, in Oglethorpe County, should be
brought to Auraria. In 1846 she made the trip to Lexington
and brought back the remains of her Revolutionary soldier
and deposited them in the hillside graveyard, and over the
grave a son erected a monument to commemorate the spot —
the same monument to serve also for Grandma Paschal when
more than twenty years later she passed on.[17]

But the first tenant to take the long sleep in the graveyard
was a stranger, whose resting place was to be marked only
by a rough stone picked up in the vicinity. Charitable
Aurarians dug the grave, and when it began to appear to
the man with the cart, who had brought the corpse, that he
also was expected to be as charitable as those who had dug
the grave, he objected, "Not so fast. That body can't go
until my two dollars are paid for hauling it."[18]

The log church which Grandma Paschal had erected was
so flimsily built that after one year it fell down. Then
Grandma Paschal gave over the dining room of her tavern
each week for services. Also she organized a Sunday school.
There was no resident preacher, but an itinerant happened

along occasionally and a Baptist clergyman from Hall County came up once a month. At this time there was also a Methodist congregation organized, and by 1840 there were both a Baptist and a Methodist church structure in Auraria.[19]

A poet (not Billy) wrote:

> Rave not to me of your sparkling wine,
> Bid not for me the goblet shine;
> My soul is athirst for a draft more rare,
> A gush of pure free Mountain Air.[20]

If Grandma Paschal had been a poetess she could have written these lines, or the following ones, with which she thoroughly agreed:

> Whiskey is the greatest curse,
> To soul, to body, and to purse,
> Pandora's Box holds nothing worse,
> Than whiskey.[21]

Grandma Paschal had good reason to hate whiskey, for it made miners drunk, and drunken miners boisterously broke up church gatherings occasionally. In fact the churches closed for a time their activities and the more devout members went out into the country to worship with congregations there. As George W. Paschal remembered, years later, the devout Aurarians at one period in the town's history were afraid to mention the name of Jesus.[22] Garnett Andrews, who occasionally visited Auraria on legal business, remembered how the miners came into the villages (having no doubt Auraria in mind, but not identifying it) on Saturday and spent that day and Sunday drinking and gambling. One Sunday morning, a visiting preacher happening up on a gang of gamblers, induced the leader to intercede for the parson to do a little preaching; whereupon the leader mounted an empty rum cask and shouted, "Oh yes! oh, yes! oh, yes, chuck-luck will be adjourned for half an hour to let the stranger preach!"[23]

There was some feeling in the Aurarian country that the

Georgia church organizations themselves were somewhat to blame for the low state of religion that prevailed in Auraria and thereabouts. Why had they not detailed preachers to the Cherokee country? Why did they think that a few causal itinerant Men of God happening along were sufficient? The Methodist had no resident minister nearer to Auraria than the Reverend William Culverhouse down in Habersham County. And there was the Chestatee Mission, even farther away, but the Georgia Conference, meeting in LaGrange, in January 1833, had found no one to go there and had left it "to be supplied."[24]

George W. Paschal, a Baptist, gave vent to his feelings on the situation, when he wrote a complaining letter to the *Christian Index,* a Baptist paper, published in Washington, Wilkes County. "There were [are] several thousand persons residing in this county [Lumpkin], and not one Minister of the gospel," he declared. And what was worse, he exclaimed that "so far as gospel preaching has any influence, the people of this country are as destitute as the savage!" There was one house in Auraria "built for public worship," a Baptist church, but without a resident preacher, and a Methodist congregation had been formed, which had neither house nor preacher. The "wicked one increases his ranks and public morals suffer much."[25]

"Amicus Veri," who was willing to divulge his real name when anyone who wanted to know it could satisfy him "that his motives for demanding it, were any other than the gratification of idle curiosity,"[26] came hotly to the defense of Auraria. He accused Paschal of seeking cheap publicity at the expense of the fair name of the town in which he lived: "I should be loth to engage in a controversy with one who has shown himself so public spirited as to appear before the public *vero nomine* and endeavors to awaken the sympathies of the religious community *abroad,* in behalf of the *destitute white savages at home;* and I should not now notice the effusion of the gentleman's prolific imagination, if it were

not that already have our town and county, suffered from
the misrepresentations of the malicious, or from the desire
of figuring like the gentleman, in the columns of a Newspaper." Amicus Veri claimed that he knew of at least four
resident clergymen in the county, and he had no doubt that
there were at least a dozen; and one of them Paschal should
not forget — "one of the ablest Methodist denomination, who
resides not three hundred yards from the gentleman's own
domicil, and if he would put himself to a little trouble, he
might hear from him every Sabbath, as good a sermon as
he himself could preach. . . ."[27] Amicus Veri did not make
the positive statement that these four or a dozen "clergymen"
were interested in garnering the souls of the wicked more
than in searching out gold nuggets; and all indications and
bits of evidence point to the probability that any such
"clergymen" were not ordained preachers but merely gold
diggers with a certain flair for the Bible. Paschal answered
Amicus Veri effectively and in a dignified manner, adding,
"It was said the other day by a minister in this place, and
that too in the pulpit, that our place seemed to be infested
with *demons.*"[28]

Though resident ministers were slow in making their way
into the Cherokee country, that great institution, about as
much social as religious, called a camp meeting, was announced for the fall of 1833. It was to be held at the Chestatee Mission, unsupplied with a minister this year, over in
Cass County in the Oothcaloga Valley. "Such Preachers of
the Gospel, as feel willing to labor for the advancement of
the cause of Religion," were "affectionately requested to
'come over and help us.' "[29] From Auraria to Oothcaloga
Valley was no distance at all for those who were religiously
inclined or who were "out to meet folks and have a good
time."

> And to Camp Meetin's oft you go;
> You see the folks, you hear the spouting,
> You sing the hymns, and join the shouting;

> Well, for the folks, the noise and *eatin,*
> This bangs the greatest of Camp Meetin.

In the last line the poet was writing of Auraria.

The votaries of education were less loud and even less able to create excitement in their field than those of religion, in theirs. Schools were little mentioned and less cared for in Auraria, and one important reason for this fact was that most of the people in the Auraria country were men or boys beyond the school age of those times — all looking for gold instead of education or religion. It would be some years before the population of this region would become settled sufficiently to raise children for schools, or themselves to have time to become interested in religion. But there were educated people in Auraria just as there were religious people, and at least one was singled out in 1834 by the University of Georgia and awarded an honorary degree of Master of Arts. He was Joseph B. Shaw, doubtless a relative of O. P. Shaw, proprietor of the *Western Herald,* who resided in Athens, the seat of the University.[30]

And whether the University expected recruits for the student body from Auraria or not, William L. Mitchell, Secretary of the Faculty, thought warranted the expense of running an announcement in the *Western Herald,* to tell the Aurarians something about the University and what it had to offer. Any Aurarians who contemplated entering the University as Freshmen "must have a correct knowledge" of Cicero's Orations, Virgil, the Greek Testament, "Jacob's Greek Reader, English Grammar, and Geography, and be well acquainted with Arithmetic." If Aurarians did not want a severely classical education they had better not come to the University of Georgia, for throughout the Freshman and Sophomore years they must study the Greek and Latin classics, and through the Junior year, too. No information was given on the Senior year, as it was not contemplated that there would be anyone in Auraria prepared to enter so far ahead. Students during the first two years, also, regularly

attended French classes, and those who were still hungry
for more languages had "the opportunity of studying Hebrew,
Spanish, German, and Italian." Apart from the study of the
dead, dying, and prospering languages, the students had
some time left for the various fields of Mathematics, Survey-
ing, Botany, and a little History and Philosophy. Tuition
for a year was $38.00, and board "in respectable families"
ran from $8.00 to $10.00 per month.[31]

Though Aurarians did not debate the question as to
whether education should be developed from the top down-
ward or from the bottom upward, it was a practical necessity
for the student to start at the bottom if he planned to enter
the University. He must have that "correct knowledge" of
the ancient Latins and Greeks as well as of arithmetic and
other subjects; and to get this instruction he must attend an
academy. There was no such institution in Auraria, but not
many miles away down in Clarkesville there was the Habersham County Academy, where the "mode of teaching"
was "upon the new and most approved plan." It was made
"interesting to the pupil," for while he was being thoroughly taught he was "made to reason and reflect for himself, and
to feel at every step that his improvement and his success
in life" depended "upon his own exertions." The course of
study was designed to give the pupils "a familiar knowledge
of all the branches of education, and to prepare young men
for College; and at the same time give them a taste for learn-
ing and study." And as teaching school was "an important
profession," there would be a special class to receive "a particular course of instruction for that purpose." Also, the
"manners, morals, company, and habits of the pupils" would
receive "strict attention." The cost of this instruction lay
within easy reach of the children of people who could pick
up gold in the streets of their city. Board "under the parental
care of respectable families" could be had for $1.25 to $1.75
per week, and the tuition for the year was from $10.00 to
$24.00, depending on how much chemistry, languages, rhe-

toric, mathematics, and a few other subjects were taken. Probably Aurarians might have thought their own village was as beautiful as was Clarkesville, but as the academy had visions, no doubt, of attracting many more students from the uninteresting midlands and lowlands of Georgia than from the mountains, the Trustees saw fit to say that Clarkesville was "naturally pleasant; the seat of health, much resorted to by respectable strangers visiting the Mountains, Falls, Gold Region and [Cherokee] Nation."[32]

In 1833 there were probably few if any teachers in Auraria or in its hinterland, but if there were such or others mildly interested in the problems confronting the teaching profession, they were invited to be in Savannah on December 23 to attend the annual meeting of the Teachers' Society of Georgia and to enjoy the hospitalities of the city.[33] No Aurarians attended.

CRIME IN AURARIALAND

AS Aurarians took pains so often to explain, major crimes in their city were few. In the period of Auraria's greatness only one murder took place. On June 11, 1833, the *Western Herald* published this news item: "It is with painful emotions, we have just learned that ROBERT LIGON, sen. Esq. died on his way home last evening, whither his afflicted family were conveying his mangled, and almost lifeless body. His death was occasioned by a blow on the head, given by one Jesse Brown in this place on Tuesday last. On an enormity so outrageous, we forbear further comment, as the community are already sufficiently excited. Brown is safely lodged in Gainesville joal [*sic*]."[1]

Brown struck Ligon "a blow with a heavy rifle gun upon the left side of the head so violently, as to fracture the skull bone." For almost a week he languished in terrible pain when his physician recommended that he be taken to his home at New Bridge (also known as Leather's Ford) on the Chestatee where he might breathe his last among the scenes so dear to him. He died before reaching there. "If scientific skill, if filial affection, and sympathizing attention could have stayed the winged shaft of death, the aim of an assassin would yet have been defeated, and an interesting family

47

would not have been so ruthlessly compelled to change the
notes of joy and smiles of affection, for the tears of wo, and
the habiliments of mourning." So ran part of his obituary.
Ligon was a native of Virginia. He had resided a few years
in South Carolina before he moved to Georgia and settled
on the Chestatee, where he built up a valuable estate —
probably the most imposing one in the Cherokee country.
At the time of his death he was postmaster at Auraria.

Continuing his obituary, the writer added: "Mr. Ligon
for a long time had been known to our community, and
distinguished in all his dealings, as a strictly honest man.
And whilst frugality and economy marked his character, and
enabled him to place himself and family in easy and affluent
circumstances, his purse was always open to the needy, and
the stranger, and pennyless at his house always found a
home."[2]

The extent of his holdings was indicated in the notice of
the administrators' sale, held the following November. He
had horses, cattle, hogs, corn, fodder, household and kitchen
furniture, and "various other articles too tedious to mention," also "about thirty likely Negroes" and that "valuable
Tract of Land" on the Chestatee, where he lived, on which
was a "comfortable dwelling House and out houses, a good
Grist and Saw mill, and Toll Bridge across Chestatee River."
He also had a "valuable Gold mine."[3]

Brown was tried the next year and convicted of "voluntary
manslaughter," and sentenced to the penitentiary for five
years.[4]

The fact that the rest of the state was inclined to give
Auraria a bad name led people to think that all criminals
on the loose must be in or around Auraria or on their way
there. Or maybe just people who were running away from
slavery might think the fine mountain air of the Aurarian
country would be good for them and could be breathed in
safety and security from pursuers — or even slave stealers
might hope to dispose of their stolen property in the gold-
mining country, where labor was so much needed.

Notice was spread in Auraria and wherever its newspaper was read that a thief had stolen a slave from the plantation of James Chesnut, near Camden, South Carolina, and that a reward of $100 was offered for the recovery of the slave and the conviction of the thief, "and a liberal reward for the boy alone." The Negro boy, named Neptune, was about fifteen years old and "not very tall, but stout for his age," and quick speaking. It was supposed that he was stolen "by a tall sharp-faced white man, with thin small whiskers, wearing a white, or brownish Hat and Camlet Cloak."[5]

But for the most part, people were looking in the Aurarian country for runaway slaves rather than for slave thieves. William W. Balleu suffered the loss of his "Negro man named Adam, . . . about 40 years old, . . . dark complected," who talked "the Cherokee tongue." He had "a wife in the Nation at Sally McDaniels, Mother-in-law to Joseph Van." Balleu offered $10 to anyone who would deliver Adam to him.[6] A. Dauvergne, down in Gainesville, discovered one morning that his slave Harrison had run away and he offered a liberal reward to anyone who would return him. Harrison was "thick set, fond of conversation, and very familiar with those" who conversed with him.[7]

One Sunday night down in Jackson County a whole family of Negroes — a man, his wife, and their two children — disappeared from the premises of Piramus Camp. The man, named Dick but probably giving his name as McKenzie, was "common size, rather inclined to be slender"; his wife Hagar was "rather small of statue [stature], of a yellow complexion; speaks quick, but very broken, having been accustomed to the sea board." Camp did not assert that he thought these Negroes were making their way into the Aurarian country, but he thought it worth the expense of letting the Aurarians have a description of them. In fact Camp was not sure that the Negroes had run away at all. He thought they might have been enticed away "by a person of suspicious character, who was in the neighborhood about that time." The person under suspicion was "a chunky well set man, red full face, with hair of a sandy complexion, and supposed to be about 25 or 30 years of age." Camp was prepared to offer $10 to anyone who would get his Negroes back for him.[8]

Then over in Cass County, "A Negro man by the name of Jack" had run away from Charles Cleghorn, who had been working the said Negro Jack in his Allatoona gold mines. Jack probably had no intention of stopping in Auraria if he should pass that way, for evidently he did not like gold mining, because he was not allowed to keep what he found. Cleghorn thought Jack might be heading for Charleston, where he had one time lived. Jack was "pretty heavy built" and had "rather a down look when spoken to," and he spoke "slow and somewhat stammering." Jack had "a large nose" and he was "light complected, but a full blooded negro." He was "a Blacksmith by trade, . . . and very fond of spirits." Cleghorn was willing to give $50 to get him back.[9]

Not all Negroes who were advertised as runaways were supposed to be making their way toward Auraria; some Negroes already in Auraria were trying to get away from their Aurarian owners. For instance there was a "Negro man by the name of Henry," who had tired of working in Nathan Cook's gold mine on the outskirts of Auraria. Either of his own volition or enticed away by some white person, he left the vicinity and might have had in mind going back to North Carolina, where he had lived before a speculator brought him to Georgia. Henry was a tall Negro with "rather a down look, when spoken to," and he stuttered and materially changed his voice "before ending a sentence." Cook offered a suitable reward to anyone who should stop Henry and put him in jail.[10]

"A Negro Fellow by the name of John" liked cooking in Aurarian taverns, first for William Rogers and then for Robert A. Watkins, better than he liked gold-mining for W. Pinchback. So when he was put to doing the latter he ran away, and Pinchback offered a reward of $10 to anyone who would return him.[11]

Negroes running away from their owners were not the only animated parts of creation trying or suspected of trying to go to or from Auraria. There were also apprentices, bank embezzlers, horse thieves, cattle thieves, and horses and cattle themselves. George W. Brown, living in Gainesville, down in Hall County, was much upset because his apprenticed boy had run away, but to get him back he was willing to pay only 6¼ cents. William Cartright was his name and he was "an apprentice to the Tailor trade." "The said boy" lacked about five inches of being six feet tall. He was lame in his left leg, and when he "went off, he wore a blue coat, striped homespun pantaloons and a black vest." Brown then poured out his lamentations and threats: "He has ran away from every place he has lived at, before he came to live with me; and after I dressed him up, he took it in his head to run away from me about 10 o'clock on Sunday night, the first inst. I forwarn any person from employing the said runaway or harboring him, as he is bound to me by his father, and I am determined to put the law in force against any person that either employs or harbors him."[12] A little less than ten years previously another boy, in North Carolina, apprenticed to a tailor, ran away, but a much larger reward was offered for him — $10. He ran in the direction of Georgia but did not get farther than South Carolina. His name was Andrew Johnson and later he became president of the United States. Cartwright's subsequent career is lost in obscurity.

There was little chance for anyone around Auraria to prosper financially by turning up runaway apprentices at 6¼ cents each or even runaway slaves at $10 apiece; but when rewards got to be $1,000 an Aurarian might well keep an open eye for whatever or whoever needed to be brought in. This large reward was offered by the Bank of the State of Georgia for James S. Park, charged with having embezzled "a very large amount" as cashier of a branch of that bank in Greensboro, Georgia. Park had "black hair, black eyes, fair complexion," and was "thin in stature." It was thought that he might have gone to the gold region.[13]

Stealing a horse was never considered as serious a crime in Georgia as it was on the frontiers of the Wild West, for the reason that a man bereft of his horse in Georgia was more inconvenienced than sentenced to death as a person was likely to be in the West, where he might die of thirst or starvation or be scalped by Indians or burned up in a prairie fire. Now, there was Jesse Cockrum, a "Cherokee Indian in the lower part of Lumpkin County" (certainly not very far from Auraria), who was offering a reward for his horse, "a large grey" one, "fifteen or sixteen hands high, eight years old, and in low order." He would thankfully pay the reward to anyone delivering the horse and he pledged himself "to prosecute the thief to conviction, be him a white man, or Indian, if I can find him out."[14]

Milton Sanders of Auraria was not sure whether his "bright sorrel mare" had been stolen or had merely strayed away, but he was rather inclined to believe that she had been stolen and that by a man "about thirty or thirty-five years old, sandy hair, blue eyes, five feet, 6 or 8 inches high." The mare had "flax main [sic] and tail, about five years old, five feet high, with some saddle spots on her back, considerably wind-galled below the hocks of the hind legs, and newly shod all round." Sanders offered $25 for the delivery of the mare and thief, or $20 for the thief and $5 for the mare.[15]

Aurarians had a difficult time keeping up with their horses. Either the animals took it into their heads to run away or some thief rode them off. Two horses and a mare disappeared from Ira R. Foster's stables in Auraria and he was uncertain whether they had run away, merely strayed away, or whether they disappeared at the urgings of a thief. One of the horses was a bay and lean and the other was a roan "with his left hind ancle swolen." The mare was a "small grey" with her "back a little sore . . . and a peculiar catch in her gate [sic] while attempting to pace down a hill." Foster offered an ample reward to anyone who would give him information about his horses.[16] Another Aurarian, H. S.

Council, lost his mare, strayed or stolen (he did not know which), but he was willing to give $5 to get her back. He probably thought that a thief would risk returning her for that amount, because the mare's left eye was out and a lump was on her back. She had one white foot and was branded with the letters B. H.[17]

Nathaniel Nuckolls, one of the founding fathers of Auraria, deserved better luck than to lose his horse, either strayed or stolen, for the return of which he offered a liberal reward. The horse was eight or nine years old, "Branded on the left hip as well as I now recollect with a perpendicular line, three or four inches long, drawn through two half circles."[18] Martin Dobbs, at the nearby Burnt Stand, lost his bay mare, "blind in her right eye" and "a natural trotter." Dobbs, like so many others who lost their horses, was not sure whether or not a thief was involved, but he would pay anyone for any expense or trouble in informing him.[19] But John E. Calhoun, who lived on the Chestatee River close by, did not suspect anyone of stealing his "small brown Mare . . . with a long switch tail, no white marks," a fast walker, and shod all round. He thought that likely the mare did not like Georgia as well as South Carolina, where she was raised, and that she probably took the road to Clarkesville on her way back to that state.[20] And so the story went; it was hard to keep horses in and around Auraria. The owners were apparently careless in looking after their horses and too busy digging gold to watch for thieves.

As there was very little farming around Auraria, horses in that vicinity were used principally for riding or pulling wagons and carts. But the most dependable work animal was the steer or ox, where speed was not desired, whether plowing in the fields or pulling wagons. Thieves had little use for these animals, as they were of no value for riding; and no thief would risk his getaway on such a slow animal. So when people lost their steers, they never suspected thieves. No steer was advertised as "Strayed or Stolen" — only

"Strayed." Nathaniel Nuckolls was unlucky enough to lose steers as well as horses. Soon after his horse had strayed or been stolen, Nuckolls advertised that there had wandered off from his premises "a large pided [pied] work steer, with large white and red spots and a very large knot on his Jaw; he went off a few days since in company with two other work steers, supposed to be running away, one of which was of dunn color, and the other a dark brindle." They were last seen on their way toward Tennessee. The other two steers apparently did not belong to Nuckolls as he offered a reward only for the first steer.[21]

It was not a very heinous crime for a slave to run away from his master, whether he was running toward Auraria or from the town, and it was even a lesser crime for an apprentice to try to get away from his servitude. A horse homesick for South Carolina, trying to make his way back, and a steer seeking greener pastures in Tennessee were committing no crimes at all. Auraria was really not a crime-ridden spot despite the bad name that some people were trying to give it. The miners had to have some excitement after a hard week's work, and if they were noisy in their chuck-a-luck games, played the fiddle too loud, threw rocks at one another, and now and then knocked someone down with their fists — and even if all this were done on Sunday — Auraria was still not the "den of iniquity" which newspapers as far away as Charleston had made it out to be.

Auraria never assumed the attitude that some of the country's Wild West towns developed later, when they habitually called for attention and publicity — good or bad, they had to have publicity. How else could they expect to grow and thrive! But Auraria received its advertising, and in a short time after its naming it came to typify throughout Georgia and South Carolina and stretches beyond, the booming sinful mining town — this, long before there were any such places in the Great American West. William Gilmore Simms over in Charleston, South Carolina, just now beginning that pro-

lific literary career of his, was hearing about the Georgia
gold rush. He knew that his none-too-well liked acquaint-
ance John C. Calhoun was deep in the mining business on
the Chestatee River. After April 9, 1833 he doubtless was
seeing occasional copies of the *Western Herald,* and before
that he had read in the Charleston and Georgia newspapers
descriptions of what was going on in the Cherokee Nation.
All of this gave him a grand theme for his first long novel.
He was rapidly at work on it in 1833 and by December of
that year he had finished it. He called it *Guy Rivers: A Tale
of Georgia,* not signing his name as the author but explain-
ing "By the Author of 'Martin Faber.'" It was published
in 1834 in two volumes by Harper & Brothers, and immediately became a great success. He wrote on December 29,
1833: "It is a tale of Georgia — a tale of the miners — of a
frontier and wild people, and the events are precisely such
as may occur among a people & in a region of that character.
The work is finished. . . ."[22]

Simms did not identify Auraria by name, as this might
not seem proper, but he laid his scene in and around the
"village of Chestatee." The villain was Guy Rivers, a South
Carolinian who had wandered into the Georgia gold-diggings,
where he terrorized the people. When not in the "village of
Chestatee,"[23] he kept headquarters in a cave in a wild over-
hanging cliff about ten miles away.[24] As Simms had never
visited the Aurarian region, he pictured the landscape a little
too wild and precipitous but he did not overstep the accustomed limits that a historical novelist might approach in
developing the characters in his story. There was no person
in and about Auraria who approached the cunning fiendish-
ness of Guy Rivers, but so real did he become to subsequent
generations that they located his cave and made him the
liveliest part of the folklore and traditions of Aurarialand.
Fifteen years after the novel had been published, Guy Rivers
had become so real to Simms himself that he made a trip into
the Georgia mountains, to see for the first time this gold-

mining region — and in his most exhilarating moments, perchance, to meet up with Guy himself.[25]

But alas, Simms did not meet up with Guy or anyone remotely resembling him, and it seems that he did not visit Auraria. But he did wander widely through North Georgia and write to a South Carolina newspaper a series of letters describing the region he visited. Summing up his journey and his impressions, he wrote: "There are some striking pictures in the present population of upper Georgia, so far as we have seen it, that are particularly gratifying to every humane and liberal mind. The days when Judge Longstreet wrote his cock fighting, horse swapping, gander pulling, and sham fighting Georgia scenes (an excellent satire at the time) have passed and become obsolete, they have been buried in the rubbish of the days beyond the flood, and to them have succeeded those of sobriety and civility. We have been in Georgia upward of five weeks, witnessed a Commencement at Athens [University of Georgia], been among the miners of Nacoochee Valley, visited the Tallulah and Toccoah Falls, and Yonah Mountain, and travelled upwards of 140 miles in stage coaches about the country, and have never seen a drunken man, witnessed a fight, or heard even of a cock fight or gander pulling."[26]

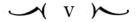

LIFE IN AURARIA

LIFE in Auraria was largely what the Aurarians made it. Though the life they led depended on many things which they could not change, yet within the ordinary limits of human existence they lived by the freewill philosophy or laissez-faire doctrines. They could not make it rain or if the rain came they could not make it quit, nor could they make the weather cool when warm, or if too cold make it hot. But they could go to church or stay away, play at chuck-a-luck and gamble away their gold or not as they pleased; they could drink clear mountain spring water or whiskey, gin, rum, and imported wines. They could go dirty or wash their faces; they could conduct themselves peaceably or throw stones at one another and fight with their fists. In fact during the early days there were fewer restraints here against freewill than in any other town in Georgia — no policemen, sheriffs, or other law-enforcing officers to be a botheration.

Billy the poet probably overemphasized the buzzing life of the place in order to produce some atmosphere, when he wrote:

> But music sure we have enough,
> Though I'll admit 'tis sorry stuff;
> And tho a trav'ler long I've been,

> A place like this, I ne'er have seen,
> Higglety, pigglety, haram, scarum,
> They keep up an eternal larum,
> And fiddle it from morn to night,
> With rastles, races and fist fight;
> And axes, hammers, billiard balls;
> Together with stentorian calls.[1]

But a poet from Milledgeville, using his imagination somewhat, called down upon his head a scolding from an Aurarian booster, when he rhymed out this:

> Wend you to the Cherokee?
>   Where the Indian girls are prattling;
> Where every one is conscience free,
>   And "chuck-luck" boxes loud are rattling;
> Where gin by the barrel full is drank, —
>   And whites and blacks are all the same;
> Where no respect is paid to rank,
>   But every one's of equal fame.

The Aurarian entered his "most solemn protest" against all this "farrago of nonsense." He admitted that Auraria had its "share of the vice and folly of the day." But he oratorically added, "The Cherokee country, it is true, has emerged from obscurity very suddenly. Where but a few days ago the foot of the rude savage roamed the greenwood and trod the verdant valley, free as the mountain breeze that gave vigor and elasticity to his frame, the plastic hand of civilization has touched the country with its wizard wand, and courthouses and villages have sprung up as it were by enchantment; and we can boast already, at least one town, of upwards of a thousand souls in population, built up for the habitations of the white man, driving a brisk trade, and exhibiting the arts and refinements of civilized life. But surely these things should not be a subject of envy to the rhymesters of the great capital of the State."[2]

One form of gambling which did not make its way to this mountain town was horse racing, though Robert Toombs and David P. Hillhouse, down in Washington, Wilkes County, would have liked to see the "stock of Southern horses" improved, whether in Auraria or Washington or all over Georgia. They announced in the *Western Herald* that the "high blooded Stallion Quidnunc," got by the "imported Bagdad Arabian," would stand in their home town of Washington.[3] The Aurarians stuck principally to chuck-a-luck.

The Milledgeville bard was undoubtedly exercising some poetic license, but not much, when he said that the whites and blacks were all the same, that no respect to rank was paid, and that everyone was of equal fame in Auraria. It was ever true that raw nature was a great leveler, and raw nature was now rampant in Auraria.

In the spring when Auraria was less than a year old, the editor of the *Western Herald,* exuberant with not a grudge against anyone in the whole world, noted how the "lofty oak" began "to spread his boughs, and cast a delightful shade upon the wary [*sic*] traveller as he" moved "in solitary reflection along the narrow trace of the savage beaten way"; the "wild minstrels of the forest, . . . continually greeting his ear with their melodious sonnets; the very air that he" breathed, "filled with perfumery more exquisite than the fragrance of Sharons [*sic*] rose, or the valley lilly"; "the surrounding romance of nature's scenery — the shelving cliffs of adamantine hardness, hung in balance by the hand of nature"; the distant hills "with pleasing magnificence, . . . and the lofty mountains decorated with that smoke like appearance"; "the winding streams," falling "in boisterous splendor over the craggy pavement" with "nature's prism" making "the various tints of the rain-bow's beauty." With a soul so full to running over, how could the editor not love everybody and everything and assert that all other Aurarians felt the same way: "It is here we find the wandering fragments of scattered enterprise from the different nations. It is here we find all ages, sexes and conditions of the human family engaged in the same pursuit. And it is here the Dandy and the Sloven will greet each other, with all the friendly feelings that the heart is heir to. It is here that the kindred social feeling exists in its full extent, connecting the people in friendly ties to the bond of union, which is calculated to inspire harmonious action, against the petty feuds that so often fester, and distract the country."[4] Indeed, if Auraria should ever change again its name, it should be Utopia!

In the midlands of Georgia, the ownership of slaves set up certain social distinctions beyond the fact that such ownership indicated a higher economic position, but the slaves in Aurarialand had to be treated more like white hired laborers, rather than as chattels to add to someone's social prestige. There were a few slaves in the town of Auraria, who did not dig for gold but cooked food in the taverns and possibly now and then acted the part of household servants in private families. Occasionally there appeared an announcement of one for sale, as in a particular instance, "a young negro man, . . . a good shoemaker and house servant, and a tolerable hand on a farm."[5]

Although Auraria had its resident population, there were many people who came and were soon gone — people who came to look after their mines, to buy mines or sell them, to engage in quick business transactions of other kinds, to see what was going on out of idle curiosity, and perchance to engage in a chuck-a-luck game and take a drink of brandy. In early July (1833) Auraria "was crowded with visitors from all parts of the United States." Among them was John C. Calhoun.[6] In fact Calhoun was a frequent visitor, as he kept a close eye on his Chestatee mines, not far away. An Aurarian news item in early May announced his arrival "directly from his residence in South Carolina," to spend two or three weeks at his mines. "And though fatigued as he necessarily was, from a long ride over the rough roads from Pendleton . . . he was yet able to sustain himself in his true character, for engaging the attention, and assuring the respect of all we believe, who had (with ourselves) the pleasure of spending the few moments that he remained here, in his company. He is commanding in appearance, easy and graceful in manner, affable, and familiar in conversation; possessing a pleasing countenance, deeply marked with all the prominent features of greatness."[7] When Calhoun remained in Auraria for an extended time, he chose to stay at Grandma Paschal's tavern, where he fascinated all who came within his presence.[8] He might well have been an attraction for already he was famous in American politics, being at the moment a United States Senator and only a few months previously having resigned from the vice presidency of the United States — an action unprecedented and never thereafter to be duplicated even into the twentieth century. At this particular time Calhoun was most talked about as the father of the Nullification doctrine, which South Carolina had applied against the tariff but had abandoned in March of 1833.

The weather was a favorite topic of conversation in Auraria, as it was everywhere else; and now and then it became news, as in the springtime when nature burst forth in the forests and woodlands and filled with raptures the heart and mind of the editor of the *Western Herald*. A snowstorm in the winter could have a like effect on the editor, even with all the attendant inconveniences. Less than a week before Christmas of 1833, the Aurarians found themselves in the midst of the thawing and melting of a six-inch snow, as they were compelled to plod their way through the muddy streets; but to the editor, who cast his eyes skyward instead of mudward: "The Mountains in our neighborhood have exhibited a beautiful appearance — dressed in the spotless robes of winter, and lifting their hoary heads, in towering grandeur, they reflect from the glittering foliage of their forest covered summits, the dazzling glories of the 'King of Day.' Nothing indeed can present more magnificent beauty, than the frost work which now so richly ornaments the leafless groves, in our mountainous vicinity."[9]

Snow storms were beautiful but they were an economic

liability to Aurarialand, for as in the case of the recent storm,
the miners had been forced to quit all operations. The approach of winter was always looked upon with some mis-
givings, for bad weather put a stop to all mining activities.
The fall preceding the winter of this big snow had been
deceiving. According to an Aurarian news item: "The
weather has been very favorable this fall, and those who are
engaged in the mining business in our county have profited
by the old lesson of making hay while the sun shines. The
nights and mornings, however, begin to remind us of the
approach of winter, that season of the year least adapted to
the business, particularly here among the mountains where
some were forced to wash their gravel last winter with heated
water to prevent the Ice from cloging [*sic*] their Machinery;
should the winter however be favorable the operations will
be more extensive than they were last spring, for a number
of those who are concerned in the business have vested so
much capital that their whole interest is involved in their
success which will greatly depend upon their constant and
unremiting [*sic*] attention."[10]

Nature often put itself on exhibition in Aurarialand more
exquisitely than in many other parts of the country, and
especially more so than in the Georgia midlands; but on
November 13, 1833, Auraria could claim no monopoly on
an amazing spectacle, which afforded conversation for a century and marked the point from which all time was measured
by old people, with the exception of the birth of Christ. This
was the day and year "when the stars fell." Editor Fambrough took full advantage of his opportunities and abilities
to describe in poetical language this display of heavenly fireworks. It was "just before the Eastern horizon was gilded by
the dawn of day," when "the whole canopy of heaven seemed
to be illuminated with what is generally called the falling of
the stars. Meteors of various sizes appeared to be bounding
and rebounding from one part of the horizon to another, and
while some of us were enjoying the splendid scenery which

nature had painted and placed before us, we have since learned that others of our neighbors, were so shocked at its appearance as to believe that the world was actually coming to an end, and that time was about to be no more." It was rumored "that many of the most profane were frightened to their knees, that Bibles had been taken down which had been almost covered in dust for want of removal from the shelves. That cards and dice were actually consigned to the flames, and that chuckluck certainly stopped in Nuckollsville for the space of one day and night. We have heard men say that they offered up their first prayer on the occasion, and we really hope from all appearances that much good has been the result of what we considered nothing more than an exhibition of the shattered fragments of Electric fluid, which may have been produced from various causes."[11]

The Aurarians were soon being informed that their great show of "shooting stars" had been seen almost throughout the whole country, certainly from Richmond to Mobile. And now that their fright had subsided they were told that such heavenly performances had been seen before, but not quite so spectacular as this one. An old-timer recalled that while driving through the country in a wagon train, one of the wagoners who had arisen early in the morning saw a large meteor shooting across the sky in great brilliancy. In half fright and wonderment he exclaimed, "Great God, the Moon's got loose."[12]

Entertainment in Auraria was not provided exclusively by nature, whether performing gently in a fluffy snowfall, or awakening the countryside with the song of birds and bedecking it in spring flowers, or flecking the heavens with fireworks; mere man came to Auraria now and then bent on nothing more than affording pleasure to the people in exchange for as much of their gold as he could get.

Such an entertainer, to attract the attention of the readers of the *Western Herald*, headed his notice in this paper "FIRE! FIRE! FIRE!" and then proceeded, "William D.

Houghton will visit Auraria next week, for the purpose of astonishing the natives with all sorts of fire doings, such as eating fire &c. &c."[13] On the day as promised, this self-confessed "great American Fire King" visited Auraria, and after he had amused his audience "with various singular and daring feats," he told them how it all was done — just simply "converting the animal fluids into vapour, and thus preventing the chemical union of the heat with the solids." It was thought that he made at least five or six new Fire Kings out of the more daring ones in his audience. But before the evening was over, he exhibited his famous "Cat O'Nine Lives" trick, which consisted of putting a cat to death with prussic acid and then bringing it back to life "by simple inhalation of Ammonia." After he had given the poison and restorative to one of the Aurarian cats, it seemed to have come back into one of its nine lives only to depart it again "in a paroxism [sic]." The Fire King, now having turned himself into Cat Man, complained that the ammonia he had used was inferior, and on applying to the cat some stronger and re-enforced ammonia, which someone had hurried out and got for him, he was able to resuscitate the feline; but so slow was the cat in returning to another one of its lives that the Cat Man had it placed out in the open air. After a while, the cat was brought back into the hall and on examination was found to be "stiff, cold, and dead," and as it now seemed futile to attempt to restore the animal, it was tossed out into the alley. But that was not the whole story — all of the cat's nine lives had not yet been used up. Let Editor Fambrough recount the last act: "But 'mirable dictu!' we were sitting in our office the next morning, when the *identical cat* came frisking into the room." The owner of the cat would swear to its "death and identity," and would likewise swear that it was "in pretty good spirits, *considering*."[14]

The normal rhythm of life in Auraria was pleasantly interrupted not only by fire-eaters and jugglers; also there were holidays and holy days to be observed. Life without Christmas would hardly be endurable; and although this day was celebrated in taverns where liquors were sold, yet the religious and more orderly Aurarians chose Grandma Paschal's tavern for this day's observance — and whenever there was a church house standing, then some parts of Christmas observance took place there. A good many Aurarians, like people everywhere, enjoyed going somewhere else for part of the Christmas celebrating — some to Gainesville, some to Clarkesville, and others to villages farther away. On Christmas of 1833 some Aurarians went to Gainesville for "a fine and well regulated ball," but many stayed in Auraria, and among them was Editor Fambrough. "Our polite friends Mrs. Paschal & Sons gave us at their commodious Hotel, a treat that would have done honor to any up-country village in the State, though provided on the spur of the moment," remarked the editor. Then gallantly he had to add: "We were surprised as well as delighted with the FAIR assemblage we met on that occasion. This is the second time the fair inhabitants of Lumpkin have been given ocular demonstration, that they might fairly vie with their neighbors."[15]

But for careful preparation and downright enjoyment, no celebration could equal that of the Fourth of July. People looked forward to it long ahead of time. In late May the news spread throughout all Aurarialand that there would be a meeting on June 1 at the church in Auraria "for the purpose of making arrangements to celebrate the approaching 4th of July."[16] The meeting, "attended by a respectable number of citizens," was held as announced, and complete preparations were made. One committee was appointed to select the orator of the day and the reader of the Declaration of Independence, another to make arrangements, and a third committee to prepare toasts. In short order, the first committee chose Isaac R. Walker for orator and Major Hines Holt to read the Declaration. Both of them accepted.[17] Then a damper was put on all these preparations by Walker announcing that the whole celebration had been called off on

account of the sale of town lots that day in a rival rising
village nearby, later to be known as Dahlonega.[18] It was no
doubt felt that land speculation would outweigh patriotism
in too many bosoms to make the Aurarian celebration a
success.

But apparently Aurarians had underestimated their own
patriotism, for the nearer they approached the Glorious
Fourth, the more determined they were to hold their celebration — their patriotism doubtless reinforced by a rising
anger against the ungenerous maneuver of their rival. So
the evening before, they resolved to go ahead; and if Walker
and Holt did not care to orate and read at the Aurarian
celebration, there were others who could do these things —
and on short notice at that, as necessarily it must be in this
instance. The next day at twelve o'clock "a large number of
citizens of Auraria and its vicinity assembled at a beautiful
spring," close by. Only the evening before, Milton H. Gathright had been secured as reader, and not until a few hours
before, was an orator found. This person was George W. Paschal, who delivered "a short but pertinent and animated
oration." Then the company sat down to "a plain but neatly
prepared barbacue [sic], . . . served up in the good old fashioned style," proving that "freedom's morsel" needed "no
dainties." When the dinner was over, the company, presided
over by lawyer Allen Matthews, assisted by Major G. A.
Parker, drank "with much spirit, animation and good feeling"
an even dozen "Regular Toasts" plus one at the end for em-
phasis and then fifteen "Volunteer Toasts." All gave elo-
quent proof of what was most on the minds of Aurarians—
patriotism, politics, controversial matters, chivalry, and so on.

As for the day itself: "Long may it continue to be the
Jubilee which now swells and animates the bosoms of millions of freemen." Then *"Thomas Jefferson* — The drafter
of the declaration of independence; alike patriotic in his life
and at his death." The *"Heroes of '76"* were not forgotten,
"Few in number, but powerful in strength, whose motto was,

Liberty or death"; neither were the *"Heroes of the late war
[War of 1812],"* for there were "Love for their patriotism,
gratitude for their services, and reverence for their names."
Another to *"Washington and Jackson* — The political Sav-
iours of our country. Reverence for the memory of the one,
and happiness for the declining years of the other. Alike
each deserves a nations [*sic*] gratitude." The company drank
to *"The Union of the States"* and added the sentiment of
approval by quoting part of Jackson's toast at the Jefferson
Day Dinner three years previously: "It must be preserved."
To *"The Army and Navy of the United States* — The safe
guards of American liberty"; and to *"Liberty of Speech,
liberty of the Press, and American Liberty* — Names cherished
and adored by freemen; hated and despised by monarchs and
tyrants." Although the company drank to a perpetual Union,
it also drank a toast to *"Georgia* — The practical champion
of State Rights." To *"Lumpkin County* — The land of enterprise, well deserving the attention of the most permanent
capitalist." But especially to *"Auraria* — A village unparallelled [*sic*] in the annals of history for population, enterprise and talents." And the final Regular Toast: *"The
American fair."*

> Without the smiles of partial beauty won,
> O what were man, a world without a sun.

Every well-regulated Fourth of July celebration had to
have its "Volunteer Toasts" (supposedly spontaneous, but
well thought out previously); and now they came. Allen
Matthews toasted Lumpkin County with the sentiment, "Let
her motto be liberty and gold"; J. Sanderlin of Savannah
offered another toast to Jackson — "The Hero of Orleans;
The brave and entriped [*sic*] warrior and the sage, undaunted
and unflinching statesman." The Fourth of July was toasted
again, by Mr. Steel, the man who had prepared the "barbacue" — a day which needed "no parade for its celebration."
And again, by Major H. S. Beech: "May each succeeding

aniversary [sic] find the Citizens of Auraria, in as good spirits
and as patriotic as they now are." Nathaniel Nuckolls, naturally present at such a celebration by the town he helped
to found, called for: "A strict adherence to the Constitution
of the United States." Captain Franklin Paschal, a son of
Grandma Paschal and a brother of George, did not forget
the *Western Herald:* "Success to its columns in the dissem-
manation [sic] of truth science and literature." David J.
Holt, a visitor from Macon, singled out this particular part
of the gold country for his toast: "The land of enterprise; a
retreat for those weary of life, and an ample field in which
the poet may find many pleasing scenes upon which he may
employ his pen." And to make this possible Colonel William
Gillespie offered up this sentiment: "A speedy extinguish-
ment of the Cherokee title, and an amicable adjustment of
Indian claims." And then the company adjourned until next
year, "in good feeling and fine spirits."[19]

Society could express itself in informal gatherings as well
as on formal occasions. There were dances and dinner parties which in themselves could be formal or informal. And
then, too, there were weddings and births and deaths and
funerals. In October 1833 there was announced the wedding
of Daniel G. Candler and Miss Nancy Ann Matthews, a
daughter of Allen Matthews and his wife Margaret. Their
first child, born on November 4, 1834, a boy, was named
Allen D. When Allen was four years old the family moved
to Franklin County, but Allen Candler grew up to be called
the "One-eyed plow-boy of Pigeon Roost." In 1898 he became governor of Georgia.[20] A month after Allen Matthews
had given a daughter in marriage, he lost a young son, two
years and five months old, named Thomas Jefferson, in recognition of the Jeffersonian State Rights principles of the
father.[21] The cosmopolitan character of Auraria's population, which was recorded in the vital notices of births, mar-
riages, and deaths, brings out rejoicings in the first two events
but sadness in the latter as bodies were borne to the grave-

yard overlooking the town: *"Died.* In this place, on the morning of the 12th inst. [September 1833] Mr. JOSEPH HOWARD, a native of North Carolina, but for the three years last past, a resident of Georgia. Mr. H. was an honest, industrious, and persevering man."[22] Others had preceded Howard, and many others were to follow.

The kind of dance which would likely leave its traces for future generations to enjoy and relive was the affair that went under the name of *Frolic,* country variety even though taking place in the City of Auraria. All that would be needed was an observer with a sense of humor and a knack at exaggeration to catch the tenor of the conversation and to develop the atmosphere of the occasion. "Juvenis Paulding," being wearied of life where fashion had established "a kind of formal refinement," where certain rules of etiquette had to be observed "in order to obtain a place among the *beau monde,*" decided to wend his way to "a little *village* in the *west.*"

Having arrived at this village (thinly-veiled Auraria), he soon learned that there was to be a frolic that evening to which he was invited on payment of sixty-two-and-a-half cents. On his way to his tavern to dress for the occasion, he heard someone ask "what gals were to be at the 'Frollick.' " The inquisitive one was answered by "a large man seven feet high," who seemed "to be rather of the giant race," who "bawled out in a thundering voice, 'my darters and old Tommy Gossip's galls, and all the galls all round about heer, and you know there's no few of um.' " When Juvenis arrived at the dance he saw the house filled with "a set as jovial lads as ever shook a *brogue* over a floor," and lassies, too. Some of this assemblage were *"shod* and some *unshod."* In one corner of the room sat "a large muscular red whiskered man, upon whose cheeks were clearly developed the premonitory symptoms of *scarlet fever,* and whose tattered elbows told, that many a *cat gut* had suffered much from his fiddle bow." Soon he announced the "regulashuns of the ball; all you what have on shoes and stockings is to go head, and them ar lads what have on stockings is to go next." And then he shouted to one of the musicians, "chune up your old banger, and give us that good old chune, Noches [Natchez] under the Hills."

And now Juvenis looked on what came next: "The grinning fiddler, with nimble elbows strikes the called-for tune, each jolly lad to his partner flies, and through the mazy dance, with cheerful hearts, light as air, they trip together. Now they lead up and down, and then alamand, all around and anon, then right and left and last of all, though not least interesting, each smiling *pair,* with shuffle hop and jump, glide through the set dance." And now, apparently someone had not been invited, for at the very height of this frolic, "all of a sudden was heard against the sides and top of the house, rap, rap, rap, a volley of stones, in quick succession as the falling of hail stones. Consternation for a moment seized the inmates, and all was as still as the midnight slumber." The manager of the dance "leaped into the street, with gnashing teeth and quivering lips, blue with rage, brandished his pistols not a few, and in a loud, shrill voice exclaimed, 'Who throwed them ar stones? I can tar his hide into shoe strings with my panter-claws in less nor no time. Here's a rale jenuine five doler bill, to any man that'll own hit.' The moment the shrill notes of the speaker had died away, a yell was raised, at a little distance, like the Indian war whoop." At that moment Juvenis "peeped through the *chinks* of the building and saw by the light of the moon, a large, rough, uncoothed looking figure, advancing with gigantic strides, toward the speaker, and at every step bawled 'It was I, it was I, ·and now pay me the five dollars in short order, or the way I'll knock you into a cocked hat is distressin', and is nothin' to nobody. I'm the boy what can jump over mountains, and tar up black-jacks, tumble rocks, as big as a mill house, into the river, and skin slash, ten of the best men, that ever trod shoe luther, whoo-p-e, now go it Jerry, all on the six!!!' "

For a moment there was a "smuthered hum," and then an outburst like the roar of a lion. Now the frolic manager "in a calm smooth under tone" asked, "Why *Bob,* was it you?" And then came the reply, "Too — be-shore, in sartin it was, you infarnal, tarnashun, gumpshus *mud-lugger,* and now pay me, or the way I'll ware you out is a rale candid fact, and a sin to Krokit." The money was quickly handed over and the dance resumed.

At this stage of the proceedings Juvenis decided that it was about time for him to get a hand and a foot into the frolic. Time after time he tried to capture one of "the galls," but they all eluded him. He now appealed to the manager for help, who replied, "Stranger, you don't know how to ax um, you must ax um three or four times, and ef they do'nt come, jist kitch um by their paws, and drag um out." And showing how it was done, the manager "wheeled round and addressed a stout plump face young lady, 'You sal! come along heer and dance with this Stranger.' 'What fur Jim,' she drily answered, and at the same time, threw her head to one side, and rolled up her blue eyes and placed them in a fixed gaze upon me. 'Just because I wa'nt you to,' he abruptly answered. 'Well, I reckon you need'nt git mad or nuthin so Jimmy.' 'Here Sis,' continued the shy lass, 'hold my cake teel I hop a jig with this heer man.'" Now the manager turned to Juvenis and said, "mister go ahead, old feginny [Virginia] never tire, by gum."

As Juvenis recounted the next act: "The musick commenced, and werily we tripped together, through the various changes of the dance. But alas! pleasure never comes unaloyed." Apparently mischievous Aurarians on the outside, probably some who had been unable to raise the sixty-two-and-a-half cents, had concluded that the frolic had gone far enough. "Suddenly a tremendous noise, as of a mighty cannonade burst upon our ears," Juvenis continued. "Bang!!! bang!!! bang!!! ten thousand *matches* were heard without and within the ball-room. Instantly the house was filled with lighted torches; peel after peel, the matches continued, until the room was in one entire blaze of fire. The ladies screamed and squalled for mercy, the gentlemen bawled lustily for quarters. This only increased the energies of the assailants. All now was one entire motly [sic] heap of confusion and disorder within. I verily thought old Hickory had fallen upon us for a band of South Carolina Nullifiers, and was reeking his vengeance upon our devoted heads, with the Cannon, he thundered against the proud Packingham at New-Orleans. To fly, for refuge, at this critical moment, was death, to stay, was to be suffocated with sulphurious vapour. I, however, resolved, come what would, to fly. And through fire and smoke, I rushed into the Street, leaving my hat and cane behind, to the victors, and through streets I flew as fast as my legs would carry me, to my lodgings, and after *cooling time* I was extremely happy, to find that I had been much worse frightened, than hurt."

Even after seeing and being a part of this great Aurarian display of social activities, Juvenis was still "convinced that Human nature, in every country" was "pretty much the same." "For in the vain circle where formal fashion" dwelled, he concluded, "more secret envy" lurked, and "more tea-table slander" was propagated, than in this lively mountain village. "But in a scene, such as I have described the same passion exists but in a more rude state, untrammeled by the refinements of fashion."[23]

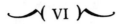

GOVERNMENT AND POLITICS

THE fact that Auraria was built on the watershed between the Chestatee and the Etowah, two rivers representing systems leading as far apart as Apalachicola, Florida, and Mobile, Alabama, had its advantages. When once this height of land had been reached, there were fewer rivers to cross in going north and south. Auraria was founded on no road or even Indian path and no Indian village had ever been located on the site of this new town; but a half dozen or more miles to the northward ran the great so-called Indian Path from the Tugaloo River on Georgia's northeastern border southwestwardly to the Coosa River in Alabama. The nearest crossing of the Chestatee to the southeastward was Leather's Ford or New Bridge, the name depending on whether the traveler had rather risk by a free crossing the swift clear currents of the river or pay a toll and cross on a bridge which Robert Ligon owned.

In Auraria's early days the part of Georgia tributary to the gold diggings lay to the southeastward through Gainesville and on to Athens and Augusta. Anyone going in this direction must cross the Chattahoochee River in addition to the Chestatee. Any crossing of the Chattahoochee below Gainesville was by ferry, with one exception. The first path to Auraria was beat by William Dean, Nathaniel Nuckolls,

and the other early pioneers; but soon it was widened into
a road over which wheeled vehicles could go and it now
became a post route to the northward.

In April 1833, Alvine E. Whitten of Carnesville, in Franklin County, over on the South Carolina border, announced
that he had put into operation a new stage line from Pendleton, South Carolina (Calhoun's home town), by way of
Carnesville to Gainesville, leaving Pendleton every Monday
morning and arriving in Gainesville every Tuesday night.
A stage left Gainesville every Thursday morning and arrived
at Pendleton every Friday evening. This route made it easy
to go from Gainesville through Pendleton all the way to
Salem, North Carolina, with, of course, various connections
there and on the way, with many parts of the country.[1]

The special significance of this stage news to Aurarians
was that they themselves could soon have these same connections; for on May 7, the Athens Stage Line informed the
public that it was extending a tri-weekly service to Auraria
by way of Gainesville, making the stage reach there on Sunday, Wednesday, and Friday mornings, and leave Auraria on
Sunday, Tuesday, and Thursday evenings. This schedule
gave Aurarians direct connections with Athens, Augusta, and
Milledgeville, and points between and beyond[2] — in other
words, "with almost every part of Georgia."[3] These connections were not only desirable to the citizens of Auraria, but
also "to those abroad, who hereafter may be drawn to this
land of many a golden dream, by its attractions or its fame."[4]

Now that Auraria was coming to be the jumping-off-place
for travel to the south, southeast, northeast, and southwest,
it must also serve travelers going to the north and northwest.
In 1834 the Auraria and Blue Ridge Turnpike Company
was chartered by the Georgia legislature for the purpose of
building a toll road to the Tennessee line, in the direction
of Athens, Tennessee. It was given permission to charge the
following tolls: for wagons drawn by four horses or oxen,
2 cents a mile; four-wheel carriages (stagecoaches and pleas-

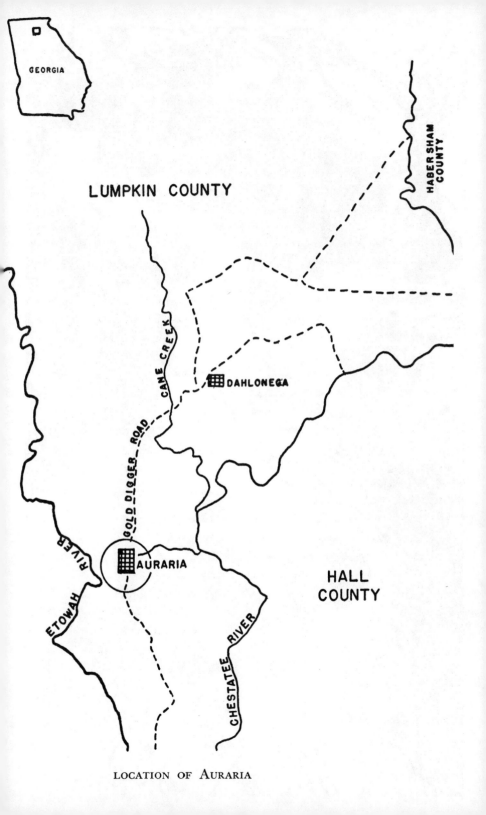

LOCATION OF AURARIA

PANNING GOLD

ure vehicles), 3 cents; wagons drawn by two horses, and all
pleasure carriages with two wheels, 1½ cents; carts drawn by
oxen, 1 cent; for man on horseback, 5 mills a mile; horse,
mule, or jack led or driven, 2½ mills; each head of cattle,
1½ mills; and each sheep or hog, 1 mill. The company was
given only three years during which it must build the road
and if it was not completed by that time, the charter lapsed.[5]
Charters were easy to get and easy to get extended. This
charter was not extended and, therefore, the road was never
built; but as the Cherokee country became populated with
white people, trails were widened into roads for wheeled
vehicles, from Auraria northward and northwestward to the
Tennessee line, passing through Amicalola, Prince Edward,
and Ellijay (or at Ellijay an alternate route through Spring
Place, joining the other route at Cohutta Springs) and on to
the Tennessee line.[6]

With these stage connections, and even before, Auraria
had its communications with the rest of the country. This
was through the mails, as mails could be delivered on horseback where no wheeled vehicle dared to go — even the two-
wheel kind. Before Auraria had a post office it was served as
a sort of branch office of Harben's Store close by, and also by
the post office at New Bridge, where Robert Ligon was postmaster, until later he became postmaster at Auraria.[7] Lawyers
in Auraria soliciting business from all who had interests in the
gold regions, announced that Auraria received mail regularly
twice a week.[8] As courthouses of counties in their infancy were
likely to be temporarily established at one place and then another before a permanent location was determined upon, mail
destined for the Courthouse town of Auraria was more likely
than not addressed simply to Lumpkin Court House, and it
would then go by way of Harben's Store or New Bridge; but
in September of 1833 Auraria received its own name as a post-
office address, and the postmaster Charles A. Ely notified the
public to address no more letters "Lumpkin Court House,"
if intended for Auraria; but all "letters intended for persons

at Nuckollsville, Harbin's [sic] store Auraria and its vicinity, should be directed Auraria, Lumpkin county, Georgia."[9]

Auraria's location on a ridge made town planning difficult beyond stringing it out in one long street atop the ridge; yet preparatory to selling off the orphans' land in November of 1833, the guardian divided it into lots and streets. On December 24, 1833 the legislature incorporated Auraria and made the town limits a perfect circle of one mile in diameter, radiating from the center of the town. With such ambitious limits, Auraria on the southwest was laved by the clear waters of the Etowah River and to the eastward it was drained by the tributary creeks of the Chestatee less than two miles away. Instead of being located only on the orphans' 40-acre lot, the town limits now included an area equal to an even dozen 40-acre gold lots with a few acres left over.[10] This shape and area for towns were not common in Georgia; and with the exception of Etowah, which was incorporated at the same time as Auraria, no towns during this period were given such limits. However, later in the century, some of the Georgia towns were incorporated with their limits a circle as much as two miles in diameter. But despite Auraria's chartered limits, it never grew beyond an elongated ridge town.

Boom towns, for whatever reasons there were for their fast growth, were always of flimsy construction, and Auraria was no exception to this rule, despite the fact that Thomas Parker, "lately from New-York," announced that he stood ready to erect public buildings and dwelling houses, "either *Stone, Brick or Wood.*"[11] Parker undoubtedly got few contracts, for some of the buildings in Auraria fell down within a year of their construction; and in subsequent years there was no evidence that any buildings were made of stone or brick. Yet, Aurarians loved their town from the beginning and wanted others to come, enjoy its prosperity, and become a part of it. One of her poets, not Billy, expressed it in this manner:

> Wend you to our town and see,
> The busy crowd all in commotion,
> The Infant town Auraria,
> Raised by Industrious devotion.[12]

When the legislature authorized Lumpkin County in December of 1832, Auraria had not yet grown up and been given a name beyond the designation, "the place where William Dean now lives." Under this name Auraria was made the provisional county seat, for here the election of county officers was to be carried out.[13] By early 1833 a full set of officers had been elected. Among those who came nearest the lives of the people were Samuel Jones as sheriff and Dr. Ira R. Foster as coroner. Dean, himself, was honored by being made one of the five members of the Inferior Court. This court immediately elected Henry Adams to be judge of the Court of Ordinary. As Auraria was only a temporary capital of the county, the governmental building, the courthouse, was only a rudimentary structure.[14]

When the legislature chartered Auraria in December 1833 it endowed the city with some unusual features of municipal government. True enough it was given the customary five commissioners, who were named in the law and who thereafter were to be chosen annually every January by the citizens of the town. The first commissioners of Auraria were George W. Paschal, George W. Bradford, Thomas Bowen, Robert Watkins, and John Thomas. One of the five commissioners was annually chosen the intendent, either by the commissioners themselves or by the citizens in the general election — the law was not explicit on this point and may have been intended to allow either method. The intendent was a sort of mayor, who called the board together and presided at their meetings. The board chose a clerk.

The unusual features of the Aurarian government related to the method of preserving law and order; but this fact should be no surprise as Auraria was an unusual town. The commissioners should appoint a marshal whose duty it was to execute all orders and ordinances of the board and he might "call to his assistance all the inhabitants of said town in the performance of his duties, whenever he" might "deem it necessary." But there were no instances recorded in which the marshal found it necessary to resort to this unusual method, for the wording of the law indicated a performance beyond the customary *posse comitatus.*[15]

Aurarians were inherently not law-breakers, whether they be permanent residents or merely sojourners for a short time. In the course of human events it was easier to leave undone those things which should have been done than to leave undone those things which should not have been done. Among a normal population it was easier not to hit a neighbor or passerby on the head with a rock, knock down an associate in a chuck-a-luck game, or stab or shoot someone, than to throw garbage out into the street and let the side drains become obstructed and stagnant water collect. Everybody's business, whether he knew it was his or not, seemed logically to be nobody's business — unless he had a very well-developed social consciousness. Since government meant to most people the preservation of law and order, the conservation and promotion of that other side of the general welfare, health, was largely a matter for individual concern.

Therefore, it was much to the credit of Auraria that six months before the town was incorporated, the first common need felt by the community was a board of health. Being located on a ridge, well drained on all sides, Auraria liked to boast of its healthful surroundings and the absence of those ailments which plagued so many other places, especially the lowlands. In May 1833, a few cases of scarlet fever were reported in Auraria, but they were light, and Aurarians were induced to believe that their "pure atmosphere" would protect them from the fatal results that occurred in other places. Yet nature could not do everything for a people's health, as "the exemption or prevalence of disease in countries and places newly settled, however healthy the climate, pure the atmosphere, or elevated the position," was not "unfrequently influenced by local causes." Aurarians decided it was the part of wisdom to do something about their local conditions which might lead to disease or even an epidemic. And now a meeting of the citizens of the town was held, with Major John Powell presiding and George W. Paschal acting as secretary. Colonel William E. Walker stated the object of the meeting and introduced a resolution in the "Whereas" part of which it was stated that "in a new, flourishing, and rapidly improving town like this, where there is no regularly constituted police, it is a consideration of the first importance that the necessary, precautionary measures should be adopted for the preservation of the public health; and the more particularly at the present time, when it is absolutely necessary that we should be prepared against an attack of that most direful scourge of the human race, the Cholera, which has been rapidly extending its ravages over different parts of the habitable Globe; and which is invited here by so many causes, produced by the immense quantities of decayed vegetable matter in our streets, the crowded state of the buildings, together with the density of our population."

For carrying out such a program, the meeting unanimously selected a committee of five, a sort of commission to govern the town along health lines, not with power to levy a tax on the people, but "raising and collecting by subscription, a sufficient sum of money, for thoroughly cleansing and keeping in repair" the streets. They were to act "as a police for, and in behalf of the town," and they were given the authority "to make and adopt such regulations" as would "best comport with the safety, comfort and health" of the citizens. The meeting recommended earnestly to the citizens that "as the surest means of avoiding disease," they use "their utmost efforts in removing everything like filth from about their houses and yards."[16] It spoke well for the fundamental stability of the Aurarians as a responsible law-abiding people that the first united action of the populace was not to organize a vigilantes committee to vent summary justice on horse thieves and murderers, but to declare war on that unseen enemy of mankind little understood then but later dubbed germs and viruses.

Work on the streets went forward[17] and in July Dr. John H. Thomas, a member of the commission (or board of health), reported that the citizens of Auraria and its vicinity were "unusually healthy" and that positively there were no cases of cholera anywhere around, irrespective of any rumors to the contrary.[18] Apparently Auraria and the immediate neighborhood got through the sickly summer months without an epidemic of any sort, but the county as a whole was not so fortunate; and this fact was disturbing to the editor of the *Western Herald,* who wanted not only Auraria but Lumpkin County as well to have a good name both in health and morals. There had been "a great many cases of fever" in the county during the past summer and fall, but the editor believed that the fever had been "produced by exposure," for he could see "no local causes in the surrounding country."[19]

Though the first love of Aurarians was gold digging, whether digging it out of the ground or from the pockets of others, yet they could not be insensible to politics — the great American game in which all could play and in which most did have a part. The 1830s, the period of Aurarian greatness, was a decade unparalleled in history up to that time — unparalleled for new ideas and isms, for fads and fancies, for emotional issues such as Nullification, Abolitionism, Cherokee Indian removal (leading to the bigger issue of state rights versus unionism), and even Davy Crockett's antics and quarrel with "Old Hickory" Jackson. And definitely a Georgia issue, of no interest or importance outside the state, but bitterly fought out inside, was the problem of reducing the number of the members of the legislature.

The continuous and most troublesome problem which excited Georgia now was the removal of the Cherokees, and out of this problem came most of the other political and constitutional issues with which the state had to wrestle. There were no Indians living in Auraria and few in the vicinity, for their holdings had already been extinguished by the purchase of their improvements. But now and then a Cherokee appeared in Auraria, as for instance the one who came to the *Western Herald* office to get his copy of the paper, and who pleased Editor Fambrough by stating that the Indians ought to move on to the West for there was little game left to hunt and that the "hunting party" to which he belonged was willing to go. The Indian said further that he realized that President Jackson had allowed Georgia to survey the land and give it over to the white settlers and that it "would be unreasonable now to stop her and force her to undo what she had done, that he did not believe the white people settled here would submit to it."[20]

Yet there was bitterness in the hearts of many Cherokees, who were determined not to move beyond the Mississippi or even away from their cabins and improvements. It was always easy to have misunderstandings about improvements having been bought and paid for. In early May of 1833, two whites who claimed to have purchased a gold lot entered upon it to begin panning for gold. A Cherokee named Bean claimed as his own a cabin on this lot, and when the whites ignored his claims, "the war whoop was raised from the house on the lot, and about twenty-five or thirty Indians all painted and undressed, rushed out and continued the yell of war, until they got in proper distance of the white men on the branch, and attacked them with sticks, clubs and rocks. The whites defended themselves with their mining tools; the contest was kept up about two hours." One of the whites received a broken arm and six or seven of the Indians were "dangerously wounded."[21]

Here was work for Major Donahoo, Indian Agent for Lumpkin County, elected by the people when the county was erected the previous year, to determine the facts and

see that justice was done. To Editor Fambrough who undoubtedly had a suspicious feeling that the white men were
in the wrong, it seemed that the laws passed by the Georgia
legislature to define the rights and to protect "the persons
and property of the Indians" were so plain that they could
not be misunderstood by anyone "unless the enchantment
of gold should direct his actions." Said Fambrough: "We do
hope for the character of the state, that no white man will
attempt to deprive the Indians of their possessions, which the
legislature of Georgia in its wisdom and lenity has guaranteed
to them until an amicable adjustment can be made with
them, by holding forth sufficient inducements to encourage
their assent to remove beyond the Mississippi, where, for
ages to come, the huntsman will find a peaceful assylum [sic]
in roaming the forest, and the agriculturalist, surrounded
with the fruits of his labour, can say in the language of a
freeman 'this is my own my native land.' "22

The Indians had been done a great disservice in the name
of kindness by the missionaries from New England and by
the politicians in Washington in attacking the good name of
Georgia and steeling the hearts of the Indians in their deter-
mination not to move to the West. The "northern inter-
medling fanatics, who were calculated to excite the worst
passions of the human soul" and the "long taught lesson of
New England's boasted notions of humanity, justice and
magnanimity," if not arrested, would "prove destructive of
the future happiness and welfare of these unfortunate people."23

The Supreme Court had the previous year declared null
and void Georgia's laws dispossessing the Cherokees but the
court had not handed down a decree implementing its decision, and Andrew Jackson had let it be known that he was
not going to act as a policeman for the court — though Georgians were not yet convinced that Jackson was on their side.
For at this very time Jackson had been going through a tussle
with South Carolina over that state's attempt to apply Nuli-

fication against the tariff law, during which time he had issued his Proclamation on December 10, 1832 declaring that
opposition to the laws of the United States would be repelled
with force, and he had signed on March 2, 1833 the Force
Bill or "bloody bill," which gave the president specific authority to call out the army and navy to enforce the laws of
Congress.

But this much Aurarians were sure of, that they had entered upon their lands with not only the permission but the
inducements of their state, and it was under that authority
that "we are here; and under which; we intend to stay here;
(the bloody bill to the contrary, notwithstanding.)"[24] And
though the "bloody bill" had nothing to do with the Indian
question, Aurarians could not be too sure about Jackson
using his troops in Georgia in some connection relating to
the Supreme Court's decision. It was hoped that he would
never "attempt to send an armed force into our state for the
purpose of coercing us into such a course of servile and
slavish degradation."

It was time to be prepared for any eventuality and to be
determined on the course to take. "Should such be the unhappy fate [of] our country," continued Editor Fambrough,
"that a decree of the Supreme Court should be made against
us on this question, and should the President send out an
armed force to drive us from the land, which our state has
granted to us, under its great seal, to have and to hold unto
ourselves, and our heirs forever; could you then possess
enough of that sort of *jugarnot* faith, to hug the wheels that
were gradually crushing your liberty; could you then kiss the
hand that administered daily, from the poisonous cup, such
a compound, as would shortly absorb your freedom and independence forever; could you then recreant like, fold your
arms in humble submission, leaving your only homes for the
chase of the savage sportsman, and march off to the funeral
dirge of your once boasted patriotism. As dearly as we love
the Union; and willingly as we would submit to its decrees,

when exercised with prudence, justice and moderation; we are not willing to see the laws of our own state repealed by a thrust of the bayonet; so long as the right of making laws is gaarnteed [sic] to the states respectively; a right which we will maintain so long as we are permitted to enjoy the soil of this country, and when deprived of its blessing, we would prefer the sod to the surface."[25]

The slightest attempt on the part of any authority to deprive Aurarians of their land would be "considered an assault," which under the laws of Georgia would "justify a battery." "And when the blow is struck," continued the *Western Herald,* "a case ensues which no Court, known to the laws of this country can determine, (no not even *the Supreme Court of the United States.)*"[26]

Every time an Aurarian saw a United States soldier or heard of any being in the state, he had visions of a tyranny being enforced against him at the point of the bayonet. In early April of 1833 news reached Auraria that a company of United States troops had passed through Athens on their way toward the gold region. Editor Fambrough did not know what object they had in mind, but he supposed that they were going on to Tennessee or North Carolina. "This much we do know," he added, "we have no use for them in Georgia."[27] Georgians elsewhere were just as excited at the news of Federal troops being in the state. It was at this time that a movement was on foot to establish an encampment in Milledgeville of "Volunteer Corps," for the purpose of promoting "Military science," and no doubt, also, to keep an eye on Andrew Jackson and to put on display for him Georgia's military power.[28] With the heading, "Be prepared for all Emergencies," a notice appeared in the Aurarian newspaper and called upon the citizens of Aurarialand to meet in May to form a volunteer corps. It ended with this admonition: "All interested in the security and protection of their persons and property, are invited to attend."[29]

It turned out that Georgia did not need to use her troops,

for Andrew Jackson was almost as determined as the Georgians were, to get rid of the Indians. In 1835 a treaty was made and ratified, removing the Cherokees to a new home in the West, and for the next three years there was the unpleasant task of collecting these unhappy Indians, many of whom were disconsolate over having at last to leave their beautiful mountain homes for the bleak plains of the Indian territory — later to become the state of Oklahoma. Collection stations were set up at various places where the Indians were held until the great trek to the West should begin. One of those stations was within a mile of Auraria. The work of removal, first begun by General John Ellis Wool and later taken over by General Winfield Scott, was completed in 1838. Aurarians and all other Georgians were glad to get full possession of their state, though many had a deep sympathy for the Indians, who by the march of time (if not of progress) were forced to go. All the other states east of the Mississippi had disposed of their Indian population already, except for a few remnants, and some states had done so by means much less humane than by forced mass migration.[30]

But in the meantime, Nullification doctrines and their application, Supreme Court decisions and their rejection, and Andrew Jackson and John C. Calhoun — all upset Georgia politics in an uncommon manner. And all of this had its perfect reflection in Auraria. John C. Calhoun often visited Auraria and his very presence radiated support and admiration for him and approval by many for his Nullification doctrine; Andrew Jackson never visited Georgia while President, but it became more evident with the passing of the months and years, that he would not support the Supreme Court in its attempts to stay the hand of Georgia against the Cherokees. But Georgians temporarily were terribly mixed up on Jackson; for though he appeared as Georgia's friend in the Indian trouble, yet he had threatened South Carolina.

It was indeed hard for many Georgians and impossible for a most respectable part of them to reconcile Jackson with a

decent respect for the rights of the states of the Union. So
there developed in the year 1833 two parties in Georgia,
based on whether they did or did not like the principles and
course of Andrew Jackson. Or, to divorce the situation from
personalities, Unionism versus State Rights. Heretofore the
two Georgia parties had had men's names as their designa-
tions, the Troup Party and the Clark Party. "But now the
era has arrived," said an Aurarian commentator, "when principles, not men are to be maintained in Georgia."[31] And as
set forth in a State Rights document, "We may be permitted
the remark, less by way of reproach than regret, that the
politics of the people of Georgia, have ever been more distinguished by a blind adherence to men and to names, than
by devotion to principles. The oldest among us have ever
been accustomed to hear the lines of party distinction drawn,
by placing boldly in front, the name of some eminent parti-
zan leader, more eminent for his management and skill, in
party discipline, than for his political integrity, or his zeal in
the propagation and advancement of sound political doctrines."[32]

George M. Troup and most of those who had called themselves the Troup Party came out boldly against Jacksonian
tyranny and consolidationism and soon took on the name of
State Rights Party. Those who had previously called themselves the Clark Party (named for John Clark, who had
moved out of the state in 1827 and was no longer alive) came
to be designated the Union Party, and sided with Andrew
Jackson. Soon the State Rights Party acted with the Whig
Party and merged with it, while the Union Party became
Jacksonian Democrats.

The leaders and chief men of Auraria became followers of
Calhounian State Rights and vigorously attacked the Union
Party members not only for what they were but especially
for their attempts to saddle the stigma of disunion sentiments
on the State Righters. They spent less time defending themselves than in attacking the Unionists; but they made it plain

that they loved the Union as much as anyone — a Union,
however, based on the Federal Constitution. They were
equally opposed to Jackson and the Supreme Court, whether
these two tyrannies always agreed with each other or not,
for they both were fast developing a consolidation in the
government which, if not stopped, would end the liberties
of the people. An unconstitutional law of Congress, supported by a president, and an unconstitutional decision
handed down by a Supreme Court, represented a tyranny
which no free people could long endure. For relief the people "petition, remonstrate, complain, beg and petition, remonstrate, complain, and beg in vain, for years and years,
till the oppression becomes insufferable." All pleas were answered with ridicule and contempt. It was thought that the
Union had been organized for the protection of all its citizens, but when this object was discarded, the Union was
"destroyed with it, and we can boast of nothing but the
name, which is hardly worth preserving, at the expense and
prostration of the rights and liberties of one portion of the
American people, for the benefit of the others." So said an
Aurarian State Rights advocate. Here he had in mind the
Supreme Court's Cherokee decision and the iniquitous tariff
with South Carolina's Nullification remedy, which provided
in such cases for the states themselves to determine what laws
were right or wrong. Who would want his state insulted by
someone saying that the case had to be taken "to the most
corrupt branch of that government, which" had "so long oppressed" the people — " (we mean the Supreme Court.)" Continuing, the State Rights Aurarian asked, "Are your constitutional, and your republican principles to be taken from
you in this way; will you acquiesce in a corrupt decision
made against you, by a tribunal, whose sectional interest and
private prejudices, you know will cause them to decide
against you; or will you judge of the infractions of the constitution yourselves, and decide for yourselves, when you
come in contact with obstacles of oppression and tyranny,

more objectionable to the American people than the two pence duty on the article of Tea, that brought about the ever memorable revolution, and which terminated in the establishment of a government, intended to be the pride & boast of freemen."[33]

Aurarians did not think they owed a great deal to Jackson just because he did not enforce the Supreme Court decision protecting the Indians. It was not because Jackson loved Georgia but because he hated the Indians. Georgia could have taken care of the Supreme Court without the aid of Jackson — and could take care of both without the aid of either one. "We do not care what name you call the oppressor." In the opinion of Aurarians, "call him King, or call him President if you please, tis all the same to us, and it is equally immaterial whether his name is George or Andrew, we are not in favor of submission to any such principles, as are contended for by a certain order of politicians now endeavoring to rise in our country, who think and say that Union & consolidation are synonimous [sic] terms; that the states have no rights, except such as the general government will allow them, and that the general government has the right to judge, and that the people are bound to stand to the decree, no matter how oppressive."[34] And this question needed only to be asked to answer itself: "Can the President, with all his omnipotence, bind a man hand and foot, cast him into prison, and whilst in that state, induce him to believe that he is free, and make him boast of his freedom?"[35]

It was unfortunate that there were people in Georgia who under the name of the Union Party supported this tyrant, "and who with the Constitution in their hands, and the magic watch word 'Union' in their mouths, would tear away the pillars that support our glorious fabric of republican liberty."[36]

In the fall of 1833 there was to be a statewide election in which two important matters were to be settled. First there was to be voted on a set of amendments to the Georgia Consti-

tution which were supposed to be an answer to the widespread
desire to reduce the number of members of the legislature
and thereby speed up legislative business and reduce the
expenses of government. A convention had been held in
Milledgeville in May to propose the desired amendments,
but what resulted was something which both of the Aurarian
delegates to the convention opposed and which Aurarians
were going to oppose in the fall election. The basis for re-
duction and the actual application of the remedy were calculated to produce the very opposite. The Fourth of July
celebration in Auraria roundly toasted Allen Matthews and
G. A. Parker, the Aurarian delegates to the convention, for
the part they played there — "They alike opposed the un-
equal measures of the late Convention."[37] And John Appleby expressed further the sentiments of the assemblage when
he offered this toast: "The Proceedings of the late Convention; deserves the anathmas [*sic*] of the people of Georgia."[38]

Those who dominated the late convention were the very
ones who now parading under the name of Union Party
were seeking to elect a governor in the fall — and this was
the second important matter to be settled. Wilson Lumpkin,
then governor, was seeking a second term. All that the State
Righters had to say against Andrew Jackson and more they
leveled against Lumpkin. As a general summing-up of his
character and performances, an Aurarian commentator had
this to say about him: "If you want a Governor who is artful,
intrigueing [*sic*], deceptive, changeable, yielding, compromis-
ing, swerving, cringing, boasting and self applauding in every
act of his life, whether public or private; a man who was
never known to give a correct opinion, or take a correct
position in relation to any matter, until he has time to count
noses, a man who is sometimes a *Nullifier*, and sometimes a
Submissionist, sometimes for *State Rights*, and sometimes for
Consolidation, you can get just a medley of contradictions
and uncertainties capped down upon you, by supporting the
present incumbent *Wilson Lumpkin*, a man who, when in

Congress, so much abused the franking privilege by puffing his own fame and sounding his own trumpet to the innocent, the ignorant and the unsuspecting."[39]

In the fall election Aurarians lost out on both issues. Lumpkin County gave a majority for Wilson Lumpkin and likewise a majority for ratification of the amendments. Wilson Lumpkin received a majority of votes throughout the state and entered in due time on a second term as governor; but Aurarians had the consolation of seeing ratification voted down in the state at large.[40]

A direct result of Lumpkin's election was the formal organization in Milledgeville on November 13, 1833, of the State Rights Party of Georgia, based on absolute opposition to the principles of Jackson's Proclamation against South Carolina and of the Force Bill, which followed. In a positive fashion, this party stood for the principles of the Virginia and Kentucky Resolutions and all that they implied in support of state rights and in opposition to consolidation of national powers. Every county in the state was asked to form a State Rights Association to be federated with the Central Association in Milledgeville.[41]

The platform of principles set forth by this new State Rights Party greatly pleased the Aurarian commentator: "The most we can say for it is, read for yourselves; and let every republican parent, teach his children to read it — and if he can bequeath no other legacy, let him leave a transcript of its principles, together with the *Declaration* of his country's independence, fixed firmly in the minds and affections of his offspring, and he may close his aged eyes in peace. The dim future shall be cheered and brightened, by the surest hopes to him, as he breathes the patriots [*sic*] latest wish to his country, '*Esto perpetua.*' "[42]

Aurarians immediately acted to form such an association for Lumpkin County, in a meeting at Miners Hall on December 4, by appointing a committee of fifteen to bring in at a subsequent meeting a constitution and by-laws. They also provided for two delegates to attend a party convention to be held in Milledgeville on the 12th. As only one of the county's two representatives in the legislature, Isaac R. Walker, was a member of the State Rights Party, it was decided that Colonel A. G. Fambrough, editor of the *Western Herald,* be the other party delegate.[43]

On December 28, the Lumpkin County State Rights Association was formally organized, in Auraria, at a meeting attended by "a large and unexpected concourse" of citizens. A ringing preamble and a short constitution were adopted, and speeches were made by William E. Jones of Jackson County, Hines Holt, Jr., and J. J. Hutchinson, after which the documents were presented for signatures and a subscription taken up to defray the expenses of issuing a thousand copies. It was a thrilling and inspiring occasion, "and no patriotic bosom that then contemplated the scene, but throbbed with delight, to see so many of the enterprising citizens of this county" subscribing to principles which the hireling press of the state "branded as political heresies, and which the American Nero swears to exterminate. Here too, was evinced a spirit, which while it is kept alive in our country, we need scarcely to fear for the future — we may bid defiance to tyrants and imperial purple, so long as the sacred fires of seventy-six, burn upon the altars of the hearts of our bravest, noblest, countrymen — who shew by the prodigality of their contributions, that their rule of practice in the present struggle, shall be 'millions for defense, but not one cent for tribute.' " The meeting proceeded then to elect the following officers for the Association: Dr. John H. Thomas, president; Henry M. Clay, vice president; J. J. Hutchinson, treasurer; and John N. Rose, secretary.[44]

For some years to come, Georgia remained almost evenly divided between these two great factions, the State Rights-Whig Party and the Union-Democratic Party, based now more on principles than personalities; but by 1850 all Georgians irrespective of parties began to calculate more seriously the value of the Union (a union with Northern Abolitionists and anti-slavery consolidationists) and from now until 1860 most Georgians drifted into the Democratic Party, which in the South had become a state-rights-secessionist party. And by 1861 enough Georgians had embraced the doctrines of the State Rights Party of 1833 to put to the test the right of a state to secede from the Union — and to defy the doctrines of Jacksonian Proclamations and Bloody Bills a quarter century after they had been issued.

AURARIA VERSUS DAHLONEGA

ALTHOUGH Auraria was the first spot beyond the gold diggings of Habersham and Hall counties, to be settled by the intruding miners, there were other regions some miles farther on where energetic mining and panning activities were centering. One of these places which gave the greatest promise of rivaling Auraria as a possible town site was on Cane Creek about five miles north of Auraria. Here as early as 1830 the sands of the creek and of the bordering bottom lands were being panned, cradle-rocked, and sifted, so assiduously that within a few years the whole region had been turned upside down — and the creek, being routed out of its accustomed channel, was wandering aimlessly about trying to find its way to the Chestatee River.

The Auraria diggings had the initial advantage of developing into a town, because mining activities had been more concentrated here and the place had been designated as the county site by the legislative act erecting Lumpkin County — even before it had a name and was merely going as "the place where William Dean now lives." Auraria had been chosen merely as a convenience for the people in fully organizing their county, and the law in nowise made it the permanent seat of government. Choosing the county site was

the right and duty of the county itself, and manifestly no
permanent seat should be selected until the lottery drawings
had been completed; for only then would the ownership of
all the lots be established.[1] The lottery was scheduled to
close in early May 1833. Making preparations for that event,
the Inferior Court, whose duty it was to make the selection,
held its first meeting on April 22, and it seems that its only
business at this time was to arrange an inspection trip to
view the various lots which might seem suitable for the county seat. They spent the next day looking for that lucky spot.[2]
And on the following day (April 24) they made their selection, only after a good deal of disagreement and wrangling.
Three lots were voted on, none of which was 664, on which
Auraria stood, but one of them was only about a mile to the
northward. Two of the judges immediately favored Lot 950
and another finally agreed, but the fourth one disagreed and
the fifth judge was absent. This lot was about five and a
half miles northeast of Auraria and about a half mile from
the diggings on Cane Creek.[3]

This decision naturally did not satisfy Aurarians, and
Editor Fambrough of the *Western Herald* offered the criti-
cism that the new location presented no "decided advantages
over the one on which this place is situated," and added that
it was "said to be difficult of access" and that there was general disagreement with the choice. One of the first objectives
in choosing a county site, the editor explained, should be to
secure "by a union of feeling, the active cooperation" of the
entire population of the county, rather than by "multiplying
inconveniences to drive any portion of its citizens to an application for a division of, and ultimately secession from the
county." Auraria was in the southeastern part of Lumpkin
County, and if the capital must be moved, then it should be
in a northwesterly direction — not in a northeasterly direction, as was the site chosen by the court, which threw the
county site still further out of balance with the rest of the
county. Aurarians were not so selfish as to argue that their

town must be made the county site: "Our object," said Editor Fambrough, "is to concentrate the energies of the county in selecting its capital, and to make it, what we one day hope to see it, rivalling the most prosperous and most favored of our up-country towns."[4]

To add to the storm of disapproval which was aroused in Auraria, two of the judges of the Inferior Court (including the one who had been absent when the selection of the county site had been made) issued a statement "To the Citizens of Lumpkin County," in which they declared that the selection made by the other three judges was "altogether ineligible, and inconvenient, being neither in a central neighborhood for the county, as it refers to place or population. Deeming therefore such a selection as has been made, one that cannot fail to give general dissatisfaction to the people of the county, not only for the above alledged [*sic*] reasons, but also, from the inconvenience and want of water." They disavowed "any consent or acquiescence" to the selection that had been made and they warned the "good citizens of this county, from purchasing lots, as no exertion will be spared on our part to have the site removed to some more central and advantageous place." This statement was signed by judges William Dean and A. K. Blackwell.[5]

As time went by, Aurarians became less and less reconciled to the choice of the county site. In early June (1833) "Many People" called on the citizens of Lumpkin County to meet at the Aurarian Church "for the purpose of expressing their sentiments respecting the location of the Court House."[6] Soon there was forthcoming irrefutable proof broken up into great geographical detail, of how many miles it was from the Cane Creek location to the various corners of the county, how many square miles were east and west and north and south of lines drawn through this location, and how impossible it would be to build passable roads to the place, without the greatest expenditure of labor. Everything worked to the disadvantage of Lot 950. And this critic, signing himself

Junius, was convinced that the choice had been made "either from an ignorance of the Geography of the county, or from selfish or interested motives."[7]

The Aurarians held high their glasses at their 1833 Fourth of July celebration, to drink this toast to "Our County Site; Conceived in sin brought forth in iniquity, cradled in corruption and located upon destruction."[8] There was additional reason for Aurarian bitterness against the new county site, for there had been treachery in the camp, it seemed. If not treachery, then turn-coatism, for the Isaac R. Walker who had been elected originally the orator for the Aurarian celebration, turned up at the celebration at the county site and acted as president, and even Judge A. K. Blackwell who had signed with Dean a protest against the choice joined Auraria's enemies in their Fourth of July celebration.[9] And hardly a more underhand and ungenerous stroke against Auraria could have been devised than was the announcement that beginning on July 3, town lots would be sold at the county site and continue through the Fourth and on for the next two days. Thus would the enemies of Auraria try to break up her celebration as well as her very existence.[10]

But Aurarians fought back not only by condemning the location of the county site, but by spreading the rumor that the person who had promised to sell Lot 950 to the Inferior Court, had got into a misunderstanding with the judges and had refused to make title. The editor of the Aurarian newspaper, however, was generous enough to report that the court had secured a good title to the lot and that the sales of town lots would go on as announced, adding "There is yet as might be expected some dissatisfaction on the part of the people in relation to the selection made by the court, though we hope they will so far be removed as to prevent any injury that otherwise might be done the county, by keeping the people in longer suspense upon the subject."[11]

The naming of this new county site created as much interest and confusion as had the christening of Auraria.

The first designation to be used which was more exact than merely a place a half mile from the diggings on Cane Creek, was Lot 950, but as the whole Cherokee Nation had been divided for lottery purposes into four sections, and as each section was divided into varying numbers of districts, and each district divided into lots as high as 1417 in the gold region — a gold lot was only 40 acres — there were, therefore, many lots bearing the number 950. So to make the location unmistakable, the first name for the place was "Lot No. 950, District 12, Section 1"; but reason dictated that no place could be given such a name except for geographical location. So, Lumpkin Court House became its first place name, having seized it from Auraria. Before May 1833, mail directed to Lumpkin Court House went to Auraria; afterwards in theory, at least, mail so directed went to Lot 950, but as a matter of fact, for months thereafter it still went to Auraria.

Lot No. 950 was just as anxious to advertise itself as being a gold mine as had Auraria — and those who knew Latin knew that Auraria meant gold mine. So the citizens of Lot No. 950 soon had themselves a name which also meant gold mine or simply gold. It was chosen unanimously by the Inferior Court in early October 1833, from the Cherokee language and its first spelling was Talonega. By the time the village got this name, it was "improving with unprecedented rapidity," and the Aurarian editor was willing to say so in those words.[12] Taking the name which the Inferior Court had given the place, the Georgia legislature incorporated it under the same name as well as it could make it out, but in the course of its transmission from Lumpkin County to Milledgeville and on to the printers of the *Acts of the General Assembly* for 1833 it was transmuted into Talonaga.[13] But very soon it was determined that neither spelling was proper, for a Cherokee Indian who had had "the advantages of a classical education" and who was "an alumnus of a Northern University" (probably the Foreign Mission School at Cornwall, Connecticut) set the people aright by telling them that the

name should be spelled "DAH-LOH-NE-GA." The editor
of the *Western Herald* commented: "Thus, many with ourselves have been deceived by the similarity of sound in the
'D' and 'T' — the propriety of the additional 'H' in the first
and second syllables, must strike those who have been accustomed to hearing the natives pronounce this word; as it
gives an idea of the Indian aspirate; separates the proper
syllables, and enables the eye at once to recognize a word,
before known only to the ear."[14]

But even all this explanation did not settle the spelling
of the name of this new rival of Auraria. Over the state,
people heard it pronounced and began to spell it the way
they thought they heard it. One newspaper, in Savannah,
spelled it Dablobuega,[15] but a little later on, in making another effort the paper made of it Tahlauneca.[16] But this was
an Indian name, and people might well be forgiven for spelling it in any way which appeared to be accurate in transmit-
ting the sound to paper — but at least this name was never
spelled in as many ways as Okefenokee, which seemed to
have set a world record in the eighty-nine ways in which it
has been spelled.[17] The Lumpkin County Court House or
Lot No. 950 finally rejected the educated Cherokee's method
of spelling the name by dropping the second H and making
it Dahlonega, and this became its final spelling — at least
into the twentieth century.

All of the glowing reports of growth that came out of
Auraria in its early days were now being used to characterize
Dahlonega — "one of the most flourishing villages of its age
in the southern country,"[18] "decidedly the most flourishing
Village in the up country of Georgia,"[19] "improving with
unparelled [*sic*] rapidity."[20] Town lots were selling fast and
taverns were springing up, such as the Indian King & Queen,
where liquors were of the best quality.[21] The town was soon
growing northward onto another 40-acre lot — Lot 951, where
sites for businesses and residences were being offered for
sale.[22] And in January 1834 the attention of mechanics was

being called to the fact that the county was about to erect a permanent courthouse on the same plans as the courthouses in Troup, Coweta, and Campbell counties, and the one then being built in Gainesville.[23]

There seemed to be only one disadvantage that was troubling the Dahlonegans: By the end of 1833 they still were not getting their mail, though a post office had been established there for several months. There was "considerable business done at this new town, and the Merchants, Miners and others" were "compelled to send better than five miles" to Auraria for their letters. The trouble was that the stage line had not yet been extended to Dahlonega because of the difficult road between there and Auraria.[24]

Dahlonega was growing up, like Auraria had done, without much town planning, as speculators sold their lots wherever the buyer wanted one. But early in the development of Dahlonega, when first the lots were being sold in July of 1833, "Verb. Sat. Sap.," "one who takes a lively interest in the beauty and prosperity of country villages" begged the people of Dahlonega "to avoid destroying their greatest ornament, to wit: the native growth of Shade trees, particularly the Forest oak, the most beautiful shade tree in our country." It had generally been the practice in clearing the site for the courthouse village "to lay the axe to the root of every tree, however beautiful, and the work of destruction went on until literally, not a shrub was left, either upon the public square, or upon the building lots of individuals." Later when the inhabitants had gained their senses, they found it a long and tedious process to repair the damage which they had done, as they suffered the burning rays of the sun. In the eyes of strangers or citizens of good taste nothing so much improved "the appearance of a village as a few well placed shade trees," and certainly nothing was "more conducive to the health and comfort of the inhabitants." He gave this advice: "Fell not a single tree upon the public square, nor upon individual property, unless compelled to do so." If some

COURTHOUSE AND SQUARE IN EARLY DAHLONEGA

of the fine old trees looked like they might be blown down
in a wind storm, they should be left until the following winter, when they should then be topped. The next spring and
summer the trees would then spread out their limbs and
afford beautiful shade.[25]

In the summer of 1833, Aurarians probably looked with
some disconsolation on the various activities of the county
government as one by one these functions were being trans-
ferred to Dahlonega. It began to happen during the month
of July. The sheriff announced on the twenty-third that his
next sales would be held at the new county site; and even
so early in its history one Dahlonegan had over-extended himself financially, for the sheriff offered for sale "to satisfy a
fi. fa." an "unfinished framed house, 30 by 16 feet, being on
the lot selected for the County Scite [sic]."[26] On the same
day Jesse L. Riley, Clerk of the Superior Court, announced
that "the office is removed to the Court House."[27] Now in
quick succession the Aurarian lawyers began notifying pro-
spective clients that they were removing to the new county
site.

The Bank of Darien now decided to centralize in Dahlonega its business in the gold-mining country, by securing from
the legislature in 1834 permission to set up a branch bank
in that growing town.[28] About this time P. Marlow, Aurarian
merchant, announced that he was going out of business and
would sell at auction all of his merchandise, including dry
goods, clothing, shoes, trunks, fancy articles, "&c. &c.," and
not being sure that this designation was inclusive enough,
he added "Also, a first rate wire twist, double barrelled Gun,
Percusheon Lock and Silver-mounted" and a "Horse good
under saddle or harness."[29] As further evidence of how many
people had left Auraria, the postmaster there advertised on
January 11, 1834 the names of 141 people whose unclaimed
letters remained in the office.[30]

The first session of the Superior Court for Lumpkin County was held in Dahlonega in August 1833; it had never held

a session in Auraria, though there had been judicial hearings
and arguments before the judge in chambers. Many petty
crimes were to be looked into and the perpetrators punished
if found guilty, and one serious crime, the murder of Robert
Ligon by Jesse N. Brown. Several Aurarians were tried for
running chuck-a-luck games and two unruly spectators were
fined $5 each by Judge John W. Hooper, for staging a fight
in open court. In September the court held a three-day
session with most of its time being taken up with the Brown
case. It resulted in a mistrial and Brown was remanded to
the Gainesville jail; Lumpkin County had not yet erected
a structure strong enough to restrain a murderer.[31] The battery of lawyers who attended this session showed how many
there were in the gold country or accessible to it and how
hungry they were for business. There were "between fifty
and sixty" — vouched for by one of them who was present.[32]

Dahlonega now continued to be the seat of justice and also
more and more the gold-mining center of Lumpkin County.
And in subsequent years, as the gold mines and streams of
Aurarialand were being worked over again by more expensive and efficient machinery and new companies were being
organized by more daring promoters, such as the "Etowah
and Auraria Hydraulic Hose Mining Company" (chartered
in 1859) and the "Auraria, Etowah and Camp Creek Mining
Company" (chartered in 1868), Auraria contributed only its
musical name and received nothing in return — not even the
offices of the companies, for they were all located in Dahlonega.[33]

But being the seat of justice, Dahlonega had its county
court days which were a great attraction for those who wished
to see justice dispensed, see their friends, and sometimes to
see who was the best man in the county — on a certain county
court day there were twelve fights going on at the same time,
just to settle that question.[34] And the United States Mint,
which was opened here in 1838, drew the gold diggers and
gold buyers to town, as it accepted their gold dust and dis-

pensed its shining coins. Alas, for Auraria! It was in neither
of these pictures.

THE DISSOLUTION OF AURARIA

LAWYERS and doctors and butchers and bakers and candlestick makers (if there had been any) and even the county government might move away from Auraria without badly crippling the town; but when, also, the town's newspaper, its vehicle of information and its propagation to the outside world and of news from the outside world in — when this vehicle rolled away, the beginning of the end was in sight. But when gold itself, the life and essence and very origin of Auraria, began to play out, and no more people came and those here began to move away, then there was absolutely no hope. But before Auraria completely faded out, exciting happenings in the West and Southwest were to have their part too in the drama. Texas and her Glorious Revolution and the discovery of gold in California and Colorado were to draw away the more daring and adventuresome Aurarians who had not already left for Dahlonega or elsewhere.

Editor Fambrough of the *Western Herald* had always been a loyal Aurarian from the time he had set up his newspaper and he was never loath to come to the rescue of the good name of the town when someone had uncomplimentary comments to make about it. But also he was not one to sulk in his tent when decisions went against his desires. The transfer of the county seat to Dahlonega was a disappointment to him, but he never in his editorial capacity showed a mean spirit toward the town. Instead, he was in the forefront of those praising its unprecedented growth and its glowing prospects for the future.

But Fambrough had for some time been planning to move away from Lumpkin County, and preparatory to that event he had secured the services of J. J. Hutchinson as editor of the *Western Herald,* who took charge of the paper on January 11, 1834. The end of the *Herald* was now fast approaching; three issues came out under the editorship of Hutchinson, and on January 31, Fambrough and Shaw announced that they had sold the paper to William E. Jones and Hines Holt, Jr.; but they made it plain that the *Western Herald* would continue to support the State Rights Party — the fact that Lumpkin County had voted for the Union Party candidates in the October election of 1833 may have had some influence on Fambrough's decision to leave the county.[1] The new editor and proprietors announced that though the paper had changed ownership it had not changed principles: "They hold to the entire, undivided, and individual sovereignty of the States."[2] Though there was a change of ownership but not of principles, there was a change of location. Hereafter it was to be published at Dahlonega.[3] It was now time for Aurarians to mourn in sackcloths and ashes. But they did not need to mourn for long until the sky brightened slightly. Their rival had scarcely got the *Western Herald* before they lost it. Within three months the paper was moved to Athens and the name disappeared into the *Southern Whig.*[4]

The *Western Herald* deserved to be remembered and its long-time editor, A. G. Fambrough, too, for it was he who made the paper a remarkable reflector of a unique period in Georgia's history — or viewing it from another angle, it was an open window through which future generations could look back and see the gold diggings in their infancy as well as in their furious fruition, and what was equally interesting, could see into the minds and hearts of these Aurarians. For a century it was not generally known that a single copy had come down through the ages. In 1934 the editor of the *Atlanta Journal* was bemoaning that fact: "But who will tell us the full story of the Western Herald or produce one of its time-yellowed sheets?" It "would now be a treasure trove to the historian and to every one interested in the old adventureful days of northern Georgia. Who will take the cue?"[5]

For a reason other than seeing their rival lose the *Western Herald,* the Aurarians might rejoice. The last issue of the *Western Herald* published in Auraria carried the announcement that a new paper was coming to that town. Its title was to be the *Miners Recorder and Spy in the West* and it was to be published once a week. Milton H. Gathright, an Aurarian from the beginning of the town, was the sole editor and proprietor of this paper. He intended to make it primarily of interest and value to the gold miners, by publishing essays on the geology of the region — the "arrangement of the different Strata of earths and rocks, forming this interesting section of country, and in which kind Gold is most usually found." He promised the best miscellaneous matter procurable, both domestic and foreign. As for politics, this paper was to be, in fact, independent of parties, the editor endeavoring "to pursue a liberal course, keeping at all times his columns open to the discussion of political subjects, which are or may be of interest to the country." As for his own views, he held the old Southern position with regard to the powers of the state and the nation, believing "that Federal encroachments, should be guarded against with vigilance and repelled with promptness." Yet in his contentions for state rights he would not "go to the extraordinary and dangerous extent of some of the politicians in a sister State; because he believes it would ultimately end in the destruction of the Government and all its Rights."

In emphasizing the independence of his paper Editor Gathright continued: "His opinions however, he considers as nothing more than the opinions of any other individual, he will therefore endeavor to act the part of a faithful Journalist without being subservient to the views of any party, leaving his paper open to the investigation of truth, and all interesting subjects *by all*."[6]

At this time there was being published at "Edahwah" or "Etowa" (Etowah) to the southwest in Cherokee County, on the Etowah River, a newspaper called the *Cherokee Intelligencer*. With the exception of the *Cherokee Phoenix,* owned and edited by the Cherokee Indians, the *Intelligencer* was the oldest paper in the former Cherokee Nation. This paper now decided to move to Auraria where it was to be edited by Gathright and Howell Cobb, a former resident of Etowah and not to be confused with Howell Cobb of Houston County or the most famous of all the Howell Cobbs, who was now a student in the State University. The *Intelligencer* was, in fact, combined with the *Miners Recorder and Spy in the West,* and never appeared in Auraria under its former name.[7] But Auraria's days were numbered and no newspaper could rescue it or was willing to spend much time trying. The drawing powers of Dahlonega were too great. After a year in Auraria, the *Miners Recorder and Spy in the West* moved to the county seat, and thenceforth and forever more to its disappearing days Auraria was to have never again a newspaper.[8]

Auraria was a phenomenon. Excitement had produced it; excitement was to end it. Another phenomenon had begun to develop in the northeastern province of Mexico, even before Auraria had emerged, and had begun to attract much wider attention than Auraria ever was to do. Americans were going into the province of Texas in great numbers at the invitation of Mexico, but soon they were finding many good reasons for throwing off Mexican rule, among them being Mexico's joining Texas to Coahuila, making the Province of Texas and Coahuila, in which the Mexicans in Coahuila

outvoted the Americans in Texas. In 1833, at the very time
Auraria was growing strong, the Texans held a convention,
whose chief purpose was to secure the separation of Texas
from Coahuila into an independent province of Mexico — a
step toward final independence as a republic. The *Western
Herald* felt that Aurarians were sufficiently interested in
Texan affairs as to want to read this constitution; and so it
printed a large part of it and a description of the rest.[9] Rela-
tionship between Texas and Mexico went from bad to worse,
resulting in 1836 in the massacre at Goliad of the entire
Texas forces of about three hundred men, most of them
Georgians, led by a Georgian, James W. Fannin. This out-
rage greatly excited Aurarians and upset them. A company
of Aurarians immediately organized and set out for Texas,
with Franklin Paschal, a son of Grandma Paschal, as lieu-
tenant. The kind of men who left Auraria to help win Texan
independence were those staunch patriotic citizens whom the
town could ill afford to lose. George Washington Paschal
was soon on his way to the West, settling first in Arkansas,
then Texas, and after the Civil War, in Washington, D. C.[10]

During the next decade and a half the star of Auraria sank
lower but not yet to the point of setting. Early in 1848 gold
was discovered in California and by the next year the news
had filtered to almost every civilized corner of the earth.
Naturally gold-conscious citizens of Aurarialand and many
other Georgians and Americans in general heard the news
and either dreamed of going or actually set out. It was at
this point in time when Dr. Stephenson made his famous
remark, "There's millions in it," as he tried to restrain his
fellow Georgians from leaving for California. Stephenson
was not alone in his efforts to keep Georgians at home. The
newspapers of the state entered the argument but used different tactics. Instead of emphasizing what Stephenson was
saying and probably assuming that he and others were doing
well enough along that line, they began to inform the people
of the horrors and seamy side of that so-called land of prom-

ise, even if one were so fortunate as not to lose his life in trying to go there. A news item in 1852 listed thirty Georgians on one vessel, who died on their way from Panama to California, five of them being from Lumpkin County.[11] Another item the same year spread a rumor, with an air that smacked of truth, that recently the Indians had murdered 150 whites in California and stated as a fact that the "Grampus Islands, in the Pacific ocean were swallowed up by an earthquake in February last."[12] An editor entitled his advice against going to California with this heading: "California gold — Look before you leap."[13] In writing of "Things in California," an Athens editor said "The record of acts of violence, suicide, etc., are from only one number [of newspapers recently received from California] which we give as a specimen of what may be found in almost every paper published in the State," and he then proceeded to give a list.[14]

With the exodus to California, Auraria lost more of her population. Thomas Baldwin and Dr. J. Thomas, in their *New and Complete Gazetteer of the United States* published in 1854 and containing 1,364 pages, awarded Auraria four lines on a double-columned page, which contained this pertinent information about the town, "a small post-village of Lumpkin county, Georgia, . . . surrounded by a hilly region containing valuable gold mines."[15] A Southern business directory for the same year listed five merchants, including the postmaster.[16] Also for this same year, George White, one the Georgia historians of the times, found room in his *Historical Collections* to grant this recognition: "Auraria, alias Nuckollsville, is situated six miles from Dahlonega."[17]

But the gold fever had not yet run its course in enervating Auraria. If there was gold in California on the western side of the Rockies, and that fact had already been amply proved by Aurarians who had gone there, also there might well be gold on the eastern approaches of those mountains. In February of 1858 a group of Aurarians, led by the "Russell Boys" (Wm. Green, Levi, and Oliver), left for the foothills of the

Rockies, there to join throngs of others in this Pike's Peak
Country looking for the shining particles. The Aurarians
discovered gold in the sands of Cherry Creek soon afterwards
and the news of this discovery led to a stampede into the
Pike's Peak Country and to Cherry Creek, some ninety miles
to the north of the actual peak. Never forgetful of their old
mother town, the Russells named the settlement that grew
up around the Cherry Creek diggings, Auraria. On the opposite side of Cherry Creek another little settlement grew up
and the next year, 1860, the two joined hands and agreed
on the name of Denver.[18] So old mother Auraria's daughter
by wedlock changed her name to Denver, and so low had the
estate of old mother Auraria sunk by the twentieth century
that even so learned a work as *Webster's Geographical Dictionary,* published in 1949, either did not know or ignored
mother Auraria, for in listing and defining the geographical
name Auraria, it gave this wording: "First settlement in
Colorado, established 1858; soon united (1860) with two
other villages to become Denver."[19] In addition to being
guilty of ignorance or worse, the *Dictionary* was guilty also
of a mistake: daughter Auraria was not a bigamist, she married only one other village. It was the Aurarians' discovery
that led to this part of the eastern Rockies being erected into
a territory, first calling itself the Territory of Jefferson, but
being legally named in 1861 the Territory of Colorado.

There was another Georgian, named John Hamilton
Gregory or simply John Gregory, who in 1859 discovered near
the Aurarian Russells' diggings the great gold lode, which came
to be called the Gregory Lode, and the town in the vicinity
Central City, reputed to be the "richest square mile on earth."
Was this Gregory the John Gregory who lived in Auraria,
Georgia, a neighbor of the Russells, and who went to California in the early 1850s, who was in Fort Laramie when the
Russells made their discovery on Cherry Creek, and who visited them there before staking out his fabulous lode? There
is much confusion in the records and exasperating silence

after 1864 about John Hamilton Gregory and John Gregory.
Were the two men only one? The answer will probably never
be known. And in that enigma will be bound up the speculation as to whether Aurarians in addition to founding Denver
may also have discovered the "richest square mile on earth."[20]

The next great era in the history of the United States, the
Civil War, left Auraria unscathed, as far as becoming a battle-
field was concerned — General Sherman elected not to go so
far east in his invasion of Georgia down through its mountains to the seacoast. Though Aurarians were good rebel
Southerners (they had been strong State Rights men in Nullification days), joining the Confederate army did not have
the lure that gold digging had. Yet those of military age
went; and if they did not go willingly, after the middle of
1862 they went by conscription. A volunteer company passing through Auraria in the early days of the war was presented with a flag.[21] By this time, the Paschal sons had gone
their way to the West, to Arkansas and Texas — not to mine
gold but to engage in politics, journalism, and railroad building and financing. They had raised families and had sons
old enough to fight in the war. Some fought for the Confederacy and some for the Union.[22] As for Grandma Paschal,
she sympathized with the Union. But at least one of her
daughters stood by the Confederacy and showed her sympathy by participating in the flag-presentation to the volun-
teers.

George W. Paschal visited his mother in Auraria in 1858
and noted that the town had "fallen greatly into dacay";[23]
and Adiel Sherwood, who got out his gazetteers of Georgia
periodically, in his 1860 edition (the last one), did not deem
Auraria important enough to be included for a short description — he recognized it only in a list of post offices.[24] But
Grandma Paschal had by this time devoted most of her life
to Auraria and its people and she would not think of moving
away, even though all of her sons had long ago departed and
become famous. Her two daughters had married two Lilly

brothers, Thomas and John, from Virginia, then residents
of Auraria. The Lilly families remained in Georgia, and it
was in the home of one of her daughters, at Big Savannah,
on the beautiful Etowah River, where Grandma Paschal died
on October 23, 1869. She had always considered Auraria
her home, but now ninety-four years old, she in her last days
had gone to her daughter's home. Her most dutiful son
George W. had visited her in this latter place the year of her
death.[25]

Grandma Paschal was to sleep the long sleep in the old
graveyard now "desolate and neglected, on the high hill"
which overlooked the town. On the monument which
marked also the grave of her Revolutionary husband, who
had long ago been removed to this spot, was this simple
inscription:

Agnes
Paschal.
Born
June 11, 1776
Died
Oct. 23, 1869.

With the passing of Grandma Paschal the last sentimental
link with the early days was broken, and Auraria began to
sink further. A traveler passing through the place in 1879
mentioned that it also was "known by the suggestive name
of Knucklesville."[26] As Auraria neared the end of the century it also neared the end of its life. The state geologist
visiting the place in 1896 on a trip to assess the status of gold
mining and the remaining possibilities of it in Lumpkin
County, wrote of Auraria: "Now, the place is barely a shadow
of its former self. Decay has settled, like a pall, on the few
houses, left to tell the tale of its by-gone activity. A post-office
in a small country store; one or two other small stores, which,
with the first, supply the necessities of life for the immediate
neighborhood; and, probably, half a dozen small dwellings,
with a number of untenanted houses, too far decayed for

human use, is all, that is left of lively Nuckollsville of 'the forties.' "[27] There were still mines being worked in the vicinity of Auraria, one of the principal ones being the Josephine Mine, but in the days of modern machinery and transportation Auraria played no part in the economy and prosperity.[28]

Auraria having all but played out in fact, now in the twentieth century began to grow by leaps and bounds in fancy. Amateur historians in their imagination began the restoration of the place to such proportions that the Aurarians of a century and a quarter ago would not have recognized their town, could they have read these descriptions. Even so strategically situated a commentator as the Ordinary of White County, itself in the gold country, in 1930, wrote that "legendary statements" held that the first mint and the first bank "ever established in Georgia were installed at old Knucklesville — now Auraria — in Lumpkin county." The mint was later moved to Dahlonega, he said. What crimes against fact were being perpetrated in the name of legends! But fancy assisted by legend made even more flighty statements: "At old Knucklesville there was the first great mining camp in North America. The population of Knucklesville was over 4,000 at the end of 1848. Within a few days after the report came that gold had been discovered in great quantities in California," the population "dwindled to less than 300."[29] Later a visitor to Auraria with a party of sightseers declared that in its "halcyon" days it had a population of 6,000 and that now there were "just five ramshackle houses left of the glory of yesterday." He made the further statement: "Every rock in Auraria stands for a murder in old Nucklesville."[30] The "five ramshackle houses" was the only part of the visitor's description which did not appear to be an exaggeration, and according to W. B. Townsend, the eccentric editor of the *Dahlonega Nugget,* this was untrue because all of its buildings were not ramshackle. And Editor Townsend added that throughout all of his life, he had heard of but one murder committed there.[31]

In fact Auraria was an ideal law-abiding town in com-

parison with the gold-mining towns which later grew up in
the West. No vigilante committees were ever necessary to
preserve order in Auraria. Though Auraria antedated by
almost twenty years the mining booms in the West, it was in
no sense a prototype of the dance-hall, gun-shooting, saloon-
ridden mining towns which sprang up there. The fact that
Auraria was often called Nuckollsville even after it had been
properly named, led the unknowing to spell it Knucklesville
(if they could spell at all) and to think the name indicated
that the people there did a lot of fighting with their knuckles,
instead of the name referring to the fact that "old man
Nuckolls," one of the first settlers, was being honored. And
even had there been a great deal of knuckle fighting, that
would have been a mere pastime compared to the murder-
ings which made Western graveyards into "boots hills," instead of burying grounds like the respected though neglected
Aurarian graveyard, sanctified by the nearby Baptist Church,
to which it belonged.

But Aurarians themselves were not above making a good
story better. Most of what they knew about the town's history came from having heard the "old folks" talk. Memories
were ever treacherous and hearsay was unreliable and any
tale would grow by repetition. Even Simms' legendary Guy
Rivers came to be a real character among twentieth century
Aurarians. He robbed and killed in the gold-mining era and
buried his loot in a cave on the Etowah River, which the
more hardy Aurarians would point out to anyone able to
follow over the rough country.[32]

As for Auraria's rival Dahlonega, it got its start by sapping
some of the life blood of Auraria and when Auraria finally
joined the hosts of the dead towns of Georgia, Dahlonega
continued to gain sustenance from the grandeur and the
glory which were once Auraria. Tourism came to this mountain town not only because of its bracing cool air, gold panning around and about in which anyone could engage, and
its own interesting past, but especially because a few miles

away was Auraria, which once had as many people, banks, newspapers, mints, robbers, murderers, and lawyers, as the imagination of the teller cared to mention — and besides there were Guy Rivers and Grandma Paschal, with Grandma heavily outweighing Guy.

NOTES

Numbers in brackets at the top of the following pages indicate the pages in the text to which these notes refer.

CHAPTER

I

1. Andrew W. Cain, *History of Lumpkin County for the First Hundred Years, 1832-1932* (Atlanta, 1932), 106-11. Quoting the *Dahlonega Nugget,* February 19, 1897, which in turn quoted the *New York Tribune* of an unstated issue in 1897.
2. W. S. Yeates, S. W. McCallie, and Francis P. King, *A Preliminary Report on a Part of the Gold Deposits of Georgia* (Bulletin No. 4-A, Geological Survey of Georgia, Atlanta, 1896), 272. Quoting from an article in the *Atlanta Constitution* of an unspecified date in 1894. For a discussion of the early gold discoveries and the gold rush, see Fletcher M. Green, "Georgia's Forgotten Industry: Gold Mining," Part I, in *Georgia Historical Quarterly,* XIX, 2 (June, 1935), 93-133.
3. *Acts of the General Assembly of the State of Georgia, . . . November and December, 1828* (Milledgeville, 1829), 88-89. For the act setting up Cherokee County, see *Acts of the General Assembly of the State of Georgia, in November and December, 1831* (Milledgeville, 1832), 74-76.
4. *Acts of the General Assembly of the State of Georgia, . . . November and December, 1829* (Milledgeville, 1830), 98-101.
5. *Acts of the General Assembly of the State of Georgia, . . . October, November and December, 1830* (Milledgeville, 1831), 114-17.
6. *Ibid.*, 116-17.
7. James W. Covington, ed., "Letters from the Georgia Gold Region," in *Georgia Historical Quarterly,* XXXIX, 4 (December, 1955), 407-08.
8. For the 160-acre lottery, see *Acts of Georgia, 1830,* pp. 127-43. For the 40-acre gold lottery, see *Acts of Georgia, 1831,* pp. 164-67. For Cherokee County, see *ibid.*, 74-76.
9. Wilson Lumpkin, *The Removal of the Cherokee Indians from Georgia* (2 vols., New York, 1907), I, 128; Auraria (Georgia) *Western Herald,* April 16 (3, 1), 1833. The numbers in parentheses in all newspaper citations refer in the first instance to the page, and all following, to the column or columns.
10. *Western Herald,* December 14 (3, 1), 1833.
11. For an excellent contemporary description of this gold region, see *ibid.*, May 21 (3, 1-2).

12. *Ibid.*, April 9 (2, 2), 1833; Cain, *History of Lumpkin County*, 25, 42-43, 61-62.

13. *Ibid.*, April 9 (2, 5).

14. *Ibid.*, April 9 (2, 2), 16 (3, 2). A marker erected in Auraria in 1954 by the Georgia Historical Commission erroneously attributes to Calhoun the naming of the town. Powell was a professional gold miner, who had for some years operated in South America as well as in the United States. Before Auraria had grown up he had located at "Maj. Logan's, Loudsville, Habersham county." Loudsville was "20 miles from Clarkesville, and 3 from the line of the Cherokee Lands." Athens *Southern Banner*, December 8 (1, 1), 1832. Auraria was such an unusual name that people got themselves mixed up in trying to write it. Even so scholarly a person as George W. Paschal, an Aurarian lawyer, in announcing his removal to the town, called it *Aurelia*, or possibly the printer might have stumbled over the word. *Ibid.*, January 26 (3, 4).

15. *Ibid.*, April 9 (2, 2).

16. *Ibid.*, April 9 (2, 5).

17. *Ibid.*, April 23 (2, 4).

18. Savannah *Georgian*, April 24 (2, 2), 1833.

19. For example, see *Western Herald*, November 2 (1, 2, 4), 1833.

20. *Ibid.*, July 16 (2, 4). It was lot 1052, in the 12th District of the 1st Section.

21. *Ibid.*, November 2 (1, 2).

22. *Ibid.*, December 28 (2, 2).

23. *Ibid.*, September 7 (1, 3).

24. *Ibid.*, April 9 (2, 2).

25. *Ibid.*, November 30 (2, 3).

26. William P. Blake, *Report upon the Gold Placers of a Part of Lumpkin County, Georgia and the Practicability of Working them by the Hydraulic Method, with Water from the Chestatee River* (New York, 1858), 13.

27. *Western Herald*, July 2 (2, 2), 1833. A pennyweight is one-twentieth of an ounce, troy weight.

28. *Ibid., April* 9 (2, 2).

29. *Ibid.*, August 24 (2, 2); *Niles' Weekly Register* (Baltimore, 1833), XLV (September 14, 1833), 36.

30. *Western Herald*, April 16 (3, 1), 1833.

31. *Ibid.*, April 9 (3, 1).

32. *Ibid.*, April 30 (3, 4).

33. *Ibid.*, June 11 (3, 4).

34. *Ibid.*, December 14 (3, 1).

35. *Ibid.*, April 9 (2, 2).

36. *Ibid.*, May 21 (3, 2).

37. *Ibid.*, October 19 (2, 5).

38. Savannah *Georgian*, May 3 (2, 4), 1834.

39. *Acts of Georgia, 1834* (Milledgeville, 1835), 143.

40. Savannah *Georgian*, January 12 (2, 4), 1835. Quoting the Auraria *Miners' Recorder and Spy in the West.*

41. *Acts of Georgia, 1834*, p. 144. The incorporators were Alfred B. Holt, John Humphries, James P. Haynes, John Madden, Josiah Shaw, Richard S. Perssee, and John M'Leod.

42. *Western Herald*, August 10 (3, 5), 1833.

43. *Ibid.*, April 9 (2, 3).

44. *Ibid.*, January 31 (1, 1), 1834.

45. Blake, *Report upon the Gold Placers,* 13.
46. *Ibid.,* 14.
47. Yeates, McCallie, and King, *Preliminary Report,* 31-32, 266. A marker erected in Auraria in 1954 erroneously states that between "1829 and 1839 about $20,000,000 in gold was mined in Georgia's Cherokee country." It should be emphasized that even the most careful estimates involve a considerable amount of guessing as to how much gold found its way to private mints such as Templeton Reid's and Christopher Bechtler's and into trade. Matthew F. Stephenson, assayer at the Dahlonega Mint for a time and a great advocate and promoter of the Georgia gold region, estimated in 1849 that by that time 20,000,000 pennyweights of gold (in value about $20,000,000) had been taken from the Georgia mines. In the light of later careful estimates, Stephenson was greatly exaggerating the amount. See George White, *Statistics of the State of Georgia* . . . (Savannah, 1849), 393. Even three sets of tables giving the amounts of Georgia gold reaching the United States mints at Dahlonega and Philadelphia do not agree. See Blake, *Report upon the Gold Placers,* 14; Cain, *History of Lumpkin County,* 89; Yeates, McCallie, and King, *Preliminary Report,* 30-31.

CHAPTER

II

1. *Western Herald,* April 9 (2, 5), 1833.
2. *Ibid.,* April 9 (2, 2). The estimate for the county was undoubtedly too large, though for Auraria it was probably about correct, for the person making the estimate was in Auraria, whereas for the county he had to depend more on hearsay. A census taken by Georgia for the whole state, and published in 1834, gave Lumpkin County a population of 5,272. *Journal of the Senate of the State of Georgia at the Annual Session of the General Assembly,* . . . *November and December, 1834* (Milledgeville, 1835), Appendix, 56. During the first four months of 1833 "about one hundred houses were constructed at this spot, and twelve hundred persons collected: they crowded to this place to dig gold." It had grown since 1833. Adiel Sherwood, *A Gazetteer of the State of Georgia.* . . . (Third edition. Washington, D. C., 1837), 127.
3. Yeates, McCallie, and King, *Preliminary Report,* 472.
4. George W. Paschal, *Ninety-Four Years. Agnes Paschal* (Washington, D. C., 1871), 233-34; Cain, *History of Lumpkin County,* 47-50.
5. *Western Herald,* April 9 (3, 2), 1833. Mrs. Paschal & Sons also ran this same announcement in the Athens *Southern Banner,* April 13 (3, 4), 1833. It was logical to advertise in an Athens paper, as many people from this town, especially lawyers, were flocking into the gold region.
6. *Western Herald,* June 11 (3, 5), 1833.
7. *Ibid.,* June 18 (3, 4).
8. *Ibid.,* April 9 (3, 3). This same advertisement appeared in the *Southern Banner,* April 6 (4, 4), 1833.
9. *Western Herald,* April 23 (3, 4), 1833.
10. *Ibid.,* April 9 (3, 2). This same advertisement appeared in the *Southern Banner,* April 13 (3, 5), 1833.
11. *Western Herald,* June 11 (3, 5), 1833.
12. *Ibid.,* April 9 (3, 3).

13. *Ibid.,* April 9 (4, 4).
14. *Ibid.,* August 24 (3, 5).
15. *Ibid.,* April 16 (3, 5).
16. Savannah *Georgian,* August 26 (2, 5), 1834; Fletcher M. Green, "Georgia's Forgotten Industry: Gold Mining," Part II, in *Georgia Historical Quarterly,* XIX, 3 (September, 1935), 211.
17. *Western Herald,* April 9 (2, 3), 1833.
18. *Ibid.,* October 26 (3, 4).
19. Cain, *History of Lumpkin County,* 54, 85. For an excellent discussion of drovers, see Wilma Dykeman, *The French Broad* (New York, 1955), 137-51.
20. *Western Herald,* April 9 (3, 3), 1833.
21. *Ibid.,* October 19 (3, 5).
22. *Ibid.,* April 9 (2, 2).
23. *Ibid.,* April 16 (3, 5).
24. Green, "Georgia's Forgotten Industry," 220.
25. *Niles' Weekly Register,* XXXIX (October 9, 1830), 106, quoting the *New York American.*
26. Quoted in *Niles' Weekly Register,* XXXIX (October 9, 1830), 106. See also Green, "Georgia's Forgotten Industry," 220. Reid sarcastically denied that he was making big profits. In a letter to the newspapers, dated Gainesville, August 25, 1830, he explained that the "gold dust taken collectively from the mines, with the ordinary cleaning," would "lose from 2 to 6 per cent, in fluxing. Where, then, is the '7 per cent profit,' " he asked. Athens *Athenian,* September 21 (3, 3), 1830.
27. *New York Times,* October 19 (21, 5), 1933.
28. *Georgian,* February 11 (2, 2), 1835, quoting Auraria *Miners' Recorder and Spy in the West,* without date.
29. *Western Herald,* August 10 (3, 4), 1833.
30. Green, "Georgia's Forgotten Industry," 220-21.
31. *Western Herald,* November 23 (3, 4), 1833.
32. A picture of one of these notes may be found in Cain, *History of Lumpkin County,* page 52. See also *ibid.,* 76, 413.
33. *Georgian,* May 3 (2, 4), 1834, quoting *Miners' Recorder and Spy in the West,* without date.
34. *Georgian,* January 27 (2, 1), 1834.
35. Paschal, *Agnes Paschal,* 246.
36. The other members of the board were: Eli McConnell, James Liddell, W. B. Wofford, C. A. Ely, J. D. Field, and G. K. Cessna. *Georgian,* January 31 (2, 2), 1835 Cain, *History of Lumpkin County,* 76, gives a different list. See also *Georgian,* May 9 (2, 3), 1834; May 16 (2, 6), 1835.
37. *Western Herald,* April 23 (3, 4), 1833.
38. *Ibid.,* June 11 (1, 1).
39. *Ibid.,* June 11 (3, 5).
40. *Ibid.,* June 11 (4, 4).
41. *Ibid.,* June 11 (4, 3).
42. *Ibid.,* April 16 (3, 5).
43. *Ibid.,* April 9 (3, 5).
44. *Ibid.,* June 11 (4, 4).
45. *Ibid.,* October 19 (3, 5).
46. *Ibid.,* April 16 (3, 2). Editor Fambrough of the *Western Herald* gave a

stinging rebuke to those seeking gold on lands not their own: "From various sources of intelligence, we are induced to believe that a number of persons in this section of country, are daily committing intrusions on the unoccupied gold mines, by digging and other usual modes of mining; to an extent, disgraceful to such as may have engaged in this modern system of public and private plundering.

"In order to reprove the vice, it may not be amiss to apprise the ignorant if there be any such, that by the laws of Georgia, it is made a highly penal offence to dig upon any lot without the permission of the owner; and it does not matter whether the lot has been drawn or not. This much we have felt it our duty to say, in order to apprise those at a distance, who have mines here unprotected, of the importance of attending to them, as well as to notify such as are engaged in this dishonest way of living, of the danger to which they are subjecting themselves, by this new fashioned way of stealing. Confidently believing, that from the extent of the Gold Region, in this and the neighboring counties that there is room enough for all who are disposed to labour for good wages; and hope that for the credit of our newly settled, and highly favored country, that the worthy and respectable part of our citizens will use the necessary means to prevent all future complaints of this sort; by teaching those, who may hereafter be caught engaged in this business the importance of obeying the laws of the country." *Ibid.*

47. Paschal, *Agnes Paschal*, 233-34; Cain, *History of Lumpkin County*, 44. When Paschal came to Auraria he did not seem to be certain as to the name of the place. In announcing his arrival, he informed the public that he had "located at Aurelia, Lumpkin County." As there was no postoffice there at that time, he advised that letters "addressed to him should be directed to Leather's Ford, (via) Gainesville." He was ready to practice law "in all the Courts of Cherokee Circuit, and Hall and Habersham, of the Western Circuit." *Southern Banner*, January 26 (3, 4), 1833.

48. *Western Herald*, April 9 (3, 2), 1833.

49. *Ibid.*, April 9 (3, 2).

50. *Ibid.*, April 9 (3, 2). Soon Walker entered into a co-partnership with Henry B. Shaw under the firm name of Walker & Shaw. *Ibid.*, April 30 (3, 4).

51. *Ibid.*, April 9 (3, 2); *Southern Banner*, April 6 (3, 3), 1833.

52. *Western Herald*, April 9 (3, 2).

53. *Ibid.*, April 9 (4, 4).

54. *Ibid.*, April 9 (3, 3).

55. *Ibid.*, April 9 (3, 2).

56. *Ibid.*, August 24 (3, 5).

57. *Ibid.*, April 9 (3, 2); June 11 (4, 5).

58. *Ibid.*, May 7 (3, 5). This co-partnership was soon dissolved. *Ibid.*, June 11 (3, 4).

59. *Ibid.*, July 2 (2, 2).

60. *Gold & Land Lottery Register No. 49* (Milledgeville, 1833), 353.

61. *Western Herald*, August 24 (3, 5), 1833.

62. *Ibid.*, November 9 (2, 3).

63. *Ibid.*, January 25 (3, 4), 1834.

CHAPTER

III

1. *Western Herald,* April 9 (2, 2), 1833; *Southern Banner,* March 2 (4, 5), 1833.
2. *Southern Banner,* April 13 (3, 1), 1833; *Western Herald,* April 9 (1), 1833.
3. *Western Herald,* December 14 (3, 1), 1833.
4. *Ibid.,* August 17 (3, 4).
5. There were apparently three newspapers in the Cherokee country at this time, or at least two. *The American Almanac and Repository of Useful Knowledge, for the Year 1835* (Boston, 1834), 234, listed three papers in the Cherokee country in 1834, one of them being the successor to the *Western Herald* and the other two being the New Echota *Cherokee Phoenix* and the Cassville *Gazette.* It is not known that the Cassville *Gazette* was in existence in 1833, but from other sources it is known that there was a paper in 1833 going under the name of *Cherokee Intelligencer,* being published at Edahwah (Etowah), now Canton. See *Western Herald,* July 9 (3, 2), 1833; *Southern Banner,* April 13 (3, 2), 1833.
6. *Western Herald,* April 9 (3, 1), 1833.
7. *Ibid.,* April 9 (3, 2).
8. *Ibid.,* August 17 (1, 3).
9. For instance, an editorial was copied by the *Washington* (Georgia) *News,* April 25 (3, 3), 1833. The *Southern Banner,* April 13 (3, 1), 1833, said: " 'The Western Herald' is a handsomely printed sheet, of the usual size — published and edited by gentlemen of known republican principles — which, together with its location, are considerations that ought to insure it a liberal support."
10. For the great Davy Crockett craze raging in the United States in 1955, see *New York Herald-Tribune Book Review,* June 19, 1955, p. 2.
11. *Western Herald,* April 23 (2, 5), 1833.
12. *Ibid.,* June 4 (2, 5).
13. *Ibid.,* April 30 (2, 4).
14. *Ibid.,* April 9 (2, 5).
15. *Ibid.,* April 9 (2, 5).
16. *Ibid.,* July 9 (2, 3).
17. Paschal, *Agnes Paschal,* 288-90; Cain, *History of Lumpkin County,* 47. The church was not officially organized until July 13, 1833. For some unexplained reason Grandma Paschal's name does not appear on the list of those attending this meeting, although it included women; but her son George W. Paschal was on the committee appointed early the next year to select a location for the church building. Nathaniel Nuckolls seems to have been the "moving spirit" in this first meeting. He was made a deacon as well as the clerk. On a complete list of the membership compiled a few years later, Grandma Paschal's name led all the rest. Minutes of the Antioch Baptist Church in Auraria.
18. Paschal, *Agnes Paschal,* 240.
19. *Ibid.,* 246-47, 288.
20. *Western Herald,* December 28 (1, 3), 1833.
21. *Ibid.,* January 11 (1, 4), 1834.
22. Paschal, *Agnes Paschal,* 313-14.

23. Garnett Andrews, *Reminiscences of an Old Georgia Lawyer* (Atlanta, 1870), 93.
24. *Southern Banner,* January 26 (2, 4), 1833.
25. *Christian Index and Baptist Miscellany* (Jesse Mercer, ed. Washington, Georgia), December 3 (82, 3), 1833; *Western Herald,* December 14 (3, 2-3), 1833; January 11 (2, 4), 1834.
26. *Western Herald,* January 11 (2, 4), 1834.
27. *Ibid.,* December 14 (3, 2-3), 1833; *Christian Index,* December 24 (95, 3-4), 1833.
28. *Christian Index,* December 24 (95, 5), 1833.
29. *Western Herald,* August 10 (3, 5), 1833.
30. *Georgian,* August 14 (3, 1), 1834. This source gives the name as James B. Shaw; but it is written Joseph B. Shaw in A. L. Hull, *A Historical Sketch of the University of Georgia* (Atlanta, 1894), unnumbered page at end under heading "Honorary Degrees."
31. *Western Herald,* December 14 (3, 5), 1833.
32. *Southern Banner,* April 24 (1, 5), 1832.
33. *Western Herald,* December 14 (3, 5), 1833. Actually the meeting was held on December 16. For an account of this meeting see Dorothy Orr, *A History of Education in Georgia* (Chapel Hill, 1950), 122.

CHAPTER

IV

1. *Western Herald,* June 11 (2, 5), 1833.
2. *Ibid.,* June 18 (3, 3).
3. *Ibid.,* October 19 (3, 5).
4. *Georgian,* March 1 (2, 4), 1834; Cain, *History of Lumpkin County,* 63; Minutes of Superior Court of Lumpkin County.
5. *Western Herald,* January 31 (1, 1), 1834.
6. *Ibid.,* October 16 (3, 5), 1833.
7. *Ibid.,* June 18 (3, 5).
8. *Ibid.,* September 28 (1, 3).
9. *Ibid.,* September 21 (3, 5).
10. *Ibid.,* September 28 (3, 3).
11. *Ibid.,* October 26 (3, 5).
12. *Ibid.,* September 7 (3, 5).
13. *Ibid.,* June 18 (3, 3).
14. *Ibid.,* June 11 (3, 5).
15. *Ibid.,* July 23 (1, 2).
16. *Ibid.,* April 9 (3, 2).
17. *Ibid.,* August 24 (1, 4).
18. *Ibid.*
19. *Ibid.*
20. *Ibid.*
21. *Ibid.,* September 21 (3, 5).
22. Mary C. Simms Oliphant *et al.,* eds., *The Letters of William Gilmore Simms* (5 vols., Columbia, S. C., 1952-), I, 55. This news item appeared in the *Western Herald,* January 4 (3, 3-4), 1834: "it is said that a new Novel will shortly make its appearance, of which report speaks very highly, entitled 'GUY RIVERS, *a story of the South,*' in two volumes, by

the author of Martin Faber, Atalantis, book of my Lady, &c."

23. [William Gilmore Simms,] *Guy Rivers: A Tale of Georgia, By the Author of "Martin Faber"* (2 vols., New York, 1834), I, 261.

24. *Ibid.*, II, 107-08, 143-46.

25. Oliphant *et al.*, eds., *Letters of Simms,* II, 545. See also Cain, *History of Lumpkin County,* 405-06.

26. An undated newspaper clipping from an unidentified South Carolina newspaper (probably the *Charleston Evening News*), in the South Caroliniana Library, University of South Carolina. Courtesy of Robert L. Meriwether, Director.

CHAPTER
V

1. *Western Herald,* April 9 (2, 5), 1833.

2. *Ibid.,* April 30 (2, 3).

3. *Ibid.,* April 9 (4, 5).

4. *Ibid.,* May 7 (2, 5). An "Observer" after recounting the many and varied opportunities which Aurarialand held out for those who wanted to make money, addressed himself to those who might be in search of beauty and aesthetics: "To the Poet and Painter, I would say come, it is here that nature sports in her most wild and romantic gambols, and that it is almost impossible for any one of refined sensibilities, to behold our meandering brooks and mountain scenery, without feelings of pleasure and admiration; and more especially, when seeing fire in the mountains at night, which is the most grand and beautiful spectacle that can be presented to the view." And oblivious to the tragedy in such beauty, he continued, "We often behold the liquid flame, extending for miles at a stretch, and in places elevated considerable above the horizon; at others going down to the brink of some winding stream, which presented to the eye in its various positions at the same time, and receiving that enchantment which the distance lends, we are at once raised to feelings of the highest kind. — " *Ibid.,* April 23 (2, 5).

5. *Ibid.,* June 25 (1, 2).

6. *Ibid.,* July 2 (2, 2).

7. *Ibid.,* May 7 (2, 4).

8. Paschal, *Agnes Paschal,* 238.

9. *Western Herald,* December 21 (3, 1).

10. *Ibid.,* November 9 (2, 3).

11. *Ibid.,* November 16 (2, 5). The typesetter must still have been unnerved when he set his news item three days later, for he got his commas, periods, and capital letters very much mixed up. To make it easier to read, they have been straightened out in these quotations.

12. *Ibid.,* November 30 (2, 4). This is another description of the "stars falling," but without any indication as to whether at Auraria or elsewhere: "*Phenomenon.* — One of the most singular phenomena ever witnessed in this section appeared here and to a considerable distance into the country, on Wednesday last. We had not the pleasure of beholding it; but learn that about 5 o'clock, the whole heavens were illuminated with blazing meteors shooting and exploding in every direction, but mostly downwards, and presenting an appearance as if all the stars in the firma-

ment were desending [*sic*] a shower to the earth or to use the striking expression of an untaught son of Africa, 'like it was snowing stars!' which continued until half after 5 o'clock. The scene was truly awful and indiscribably [*sic*] sublime; and while it was viewed by the philosopher with admiration and delight, it carried to the bosoms of many, terror and consternation. Some imagined the world was coming to an end, and began to pray; and a gentleman from the country states that such was the alarm produced in the neighborhood where he was, the welkin every where around him resounded with cries of distress!" *Ibid.*, November 30 (3, 1-2).

13. *Ibid.*, November 16 (3, 5).
14. *Ibid.*, November 23 (2, 5; 3, 1).
15. *Ibid.*, December 28 (2, 2).
16. *Ibid.*, May 28 (3, 3).
17. *Ibid.*, June 4 (2, 3).
18. *Ibid.*, June 25 (2, 3).
19. *Ibid.*, July 9 (2, 4-5).
20. *Ibid.*, October 12 (3, 4); *Memoirs of Georgia, Containing Historical Accounts of the State's Civil, Military, Industrial and Professional Interests, and Personal Sketches of Many of its People* (2 vols., Atlanta, 1895), I, 1018-19; Cain, *History of Lumpkin County*, 54.
21. *Western Herald*, November 16 (3, 4), 1833.
22. *Ibid.*, September 14 (3, 3).
23. *Ibid.*, July 16 (2, 5; 3, 1-2).

CHAPTER

VI

1. *Western Herald*, April 16 (3, 5), 1833.
2. *Ibid.*, May 7 (3, 5).
3. *Ibid.*, April 30 (2, 2).
4. *Ibid.*
5. *Acts of Georgia, 1834*, pp. 200-04.
6. See *Bonner's Map of the State of Georgia with the Addition of the Geological Features* (Published by W. T. Williams, Savannah, 1849), folded opposite page 28 in White, *Statistics of the State of Georgia*. See also *Bonner's Pocket Map of the State of Georgia, Compiled by Wm. G. Bonner, Civil Engineer. Milledgeville. 1851.*
7. *Southern Banner*, April 6 (3, 5), April 13 (3, 2), 1833; *Western Herald*, April 9 (3, 3), May 7 (3, 5), 1833.
8. *Western Herald*, April 9 (3, 2), 1833.
9. *Ibid.*, October 5 (3, 3; 2, 1); Cain, *History of Lumpkin County*, 25.
10. *Acts of the General Assembly of the State of Georgia, . . . November and December, 1833* (Milledgeville, 1834), 332. Auraria and Etowa (Etowah) were incorporated in the same act and the same wording was used for the incorporation of each place. For instance, the limits of Talbotton were made a circle a mile in diameter in 1840 (repealed ten years later); Griffin, a circle two miles in diameter in 1843; and Marshallville, a circle a mile and a half in diameter in 1857. The limits of Dahlonega, incorporated in 1833, were by a supplementary act of 1838 made a circle one-half mile in diameter.

11. *Western Herald,* April 9 (3, 4).

12. *Ibid.,* May 21 (3, 2).

13. *Acts of the General Assembly of the State of Georgia, . . . November and December, 1832* (Milledgeville, 1833), 56.

14. *Western Herald,* April 9 (2, 2; 2, 3; 3, 5), April 16 (3, 5), 1833.

15. *Acts of Georgia, 1833,* pp. 332-33.

16. *Western Herald,* May 28 (2, 5). The following were appointed on the committee: Major John Powell, Major Thomas C. Bowen, Dr. John H. Thomas, Dr. Ira R. Foster, and William Dean. This news item appeared in the *Western Herald,* May 28 (2, 4), 1833: "*Scarlet Fever.* — We have had a few cases of this prevailing disease in our town within the last ten days. The attacks as yet have been slight, and we are induced to believe that our advantage of pure atmosphere, will relieve us from the fatal results that we hear of in other places."

17. *Ibid.,* June 11 (4, 4).

18. *Ibid.,* July (2, 2). This news item recorded the cholera rumors: "We learn from Travellers arriving from various sections, that a report is in circulation, that the Cholera is prevailing in this place. This could have originated in no other, than in a malicious or mischief·making motive, for the public, particularly, that portion intending to visit this region on business or otherwise, are assured that it is wholly without foundation. It is perhaps unparallelled [*sic*], that so large a number of persons thrown together, as the citizens of this Village have been, and the subjects of so much exposure, have enjoyed such general good health." *Ibid.,* May 21 (3, 1).

19. *Ibid.,* October 5 (2, 1).

20. *Ibid.,* April 23 (2, 4); *Niles' Weekly Register,* XLIV (May 4, 1833), 152.

21. *Western Herald,* May 14 (3, 1), 1833.

22. *Ibid.,* May 14 (3, 1); April 9 (2, 2).

23. *Ibid.,* April 23 (2, 4).

24. *Ibid.,* April 16 (3, 1).

25. *Ibid.,* April 16 (3, 2).

26. *Ibid.,* April 9 (2, 3).

27. *Ibid.,* April 16 (3, 1).

28. *Ibid.,* April 16 (4, 5).

29. *Ibid.,* April 30 (3, 4).

30. Charles W. Elliott, *Winfield Scott. The Soldier and the Man* (New York, 1937), 346; Cain, *History of Lumpkin County,* 53, 127.

31. *Western Herald,* December 21 (3, 2), 1833.

32. *Ibid.,* January 11 (2, 2), 1834.

33. *Ibid.,* November 16 (3, 1), 1833.

34. *Ibid.*

35. *Ibid.,* December 21 (3, 2). See also *ibid.,* June 18 (2, 4-5).

36. *Ibid.,* December 21 (3, 2).

37. *Ibid.,* July 9 (2, 4). For a record of the convention, see *Journal of a General Convention of the State of Georgia, to Reduce the Members of the General Assembly. Begun and Held at Milledgeville, the Seat of Government, in May, 1833* (Milledgeville, 1833).

38. *Western Herald,* July 9 (2, 5), 1833.

39. *Ibid.,* June 25 (2, 3).

40. *Ibid.,* October 12 (2, 5), October 19 (2, 4), October 26 (2, 4).

41. *Ibid.,* November 23 (2, 4).

42. *Ibid.,* January 4 (2, 3), 1834.
43. *Ibid.,* December 14 (3, 2). The members of this committee were: Dr. John H. Thomas, A. B. Holt, Hines Holt, Jr., H. B. Shaw, P. Caldwell, J. Maddin, T. C. Bowen, Robert Ligon, Jr., J. J. Hutchinson, G. Capers, Allen G. Matthews, William Lumpkin, John N. Rose, Henry M. Clay, and A. K. Blackwell. See also *ibid.,* November 30 (2, 3), December 21 (3, 2), December 28 (2, 2).
44. *Ibid.,* January 4 (2, 3), 1834. These were members of the Executive Committee: Dr. John H. Thomas, Henry M. Clay, Hines Holt, Jr., A. B. Holt, and J. J. Hutchinson, *Ibid.*

CHAPTER

VII

1. *Western Herald,* April 9 (2, 2), 1833.
2. *Ibid.,* April 23 (2, 4).
3. *Ibid.,* April 30 (2, 2).
4. *Ibid.,* April 30 (2, 2-3).
5. *Ibid.,* April 30 (3, 4).
6. *Ibid.,* June 4 (3, 3).
7. *Ibid.,* June 25 (2, 4). Later additions to the county put Dahlonega nearer the center.
8. *Ibid.,* July 9 (2, 4).
9. *Ibid.,* July 16 (3, 2).
10. *Ibid.,* July 9 (2, 3).
11. *Ibid.,* June 18 (2, 4).
12. *Ibid.,* October 5 (2, 1).
13. *Acts of Georgia, 1833,* p. 334.
14. *Western Herald,* November 30 (2, 3), 1833.
15. *Georgian,* March 29 (2, 4), 1834.
16. *Ibid.,* June 27 (2, 2).
17. A. H. Wright, *Our Georgia-Florida Frontier. The Okefinokee Swamp, its History and Cartography* (Ithaca, N. Y., 1945), I, 4-7.
18. *Western Herald,* November 9 (2, 3), 1833.
19. *Ibid.,* January 31 (3, 4), 1834.
20. *Ibid.,* July 23 (2, 2), 1833.
21. *Ibid.,* January 25 (4, 3), 1834.
22. *Ibid.,* January 31 (3, 4).
23. *Ibid.*
24. *Ibid.,* December 14 (3, 1), 1833.
25. *Ibid.,* July 9 (2, 3-4).
26. *Ibid.,* July 23 (2, 2; 4, 1).
27. *Ibid.,* July 23 (3, 5).
28. *Acts of Georgia, 1834,* p. 44.
29. *Western Herald,* October 5 (3, 3), 1833.
30. *Ibid.,* January 11 (4, 4), 1834.
31. *Ibid.,* September 7 (2, 2); Cain, *History of Lumpkin County,* 63.
32. *Western Herald,* September 7 (2, 2), 1833.
33. *Acts of the General Assembly of the State of Georgia, . . . November and December, 1859* (Milledgeville, 1860), 252-55; *Acts of the General Assembly of the State of Georgia, . . . Beginning July 4, and Ending October*

6, 1868 (Macon, 1868), 84-85.

34. Cain, *History of Lumpkin County,* 128.

CHAPTER

VIII

1. *Western Herald,* January 31 (2, 4), 1834.
2. *Ibid.,* January 31 (2, 5).
3. *Ibid.; Georgian,* March 29 (2, 4), 1834.
4. *Georgian,* May 22 (2, 2), 1834. Some Aurarians in the twentieth century remember that as children they picked up pieces of the lead type while playing on the site of the old printing shop, and that they used this lead for "fish hook sinkers." Cain, *History of Lumpkin County,* 53.
5. *Atlanta Journal,* April 29 (4, 2, in section entitled "Automobiles and Editorials"), 1934. A complete file of the *Western Herald* as long as it was published at Auraria, is extant. The first number was April 9, 1833 and the last number was January 31, 1834, being 41 numbers in all.
6. *Western Herald,* January 31 (3, 5), 1834.
7. *Georgian,* March 22 (2, 3); April 7 (2, 2), 1834; *American Almanac, 1835,* p. 234.
8. *Georgian,* August 1 (2, 3), 1835.
9. *Western Herald,* June 25 (3, 2), 1833.
10. Paschal, *Agnes Paschal,* 251-55, 267. In 1857 when Texas was about to erect a monument to the heroes of Goliad and was offering to pay for the arms belonging to the state of Georgia which fell into the hands of the Mexicans during the War for Texas Independence, the Georgia legislature resolved to make no demands on Texas, but let it become "a subject of congratulation and rejoicing to Georgia that from her bosom so brave and self-sacrificing a band of freemen went forth to fight against the oppression of their Texas brethren." *Acts of the General Assembly of the State of Georgia, . . . November and December, 1857* (Columbus, 1858), 327. Franklin Lafitte Paschal, born in Oglethorpe County, January 15, 1810, left Auraria to fight in the War for Texas Independence. Being wounded he returned to Georgia for treatment and went back to Texas in 1839, settling in San Antonio. He became the first sheriff of Bexar County. He was elected a member of the House in the Eighth Texas Congress. He died in 1884. Walter Prescott Webb *et al.,* eds., *The Handbook of Texas* (2 vols., Austin, 1952), II, 343. His brother Isaiah Addison Paschal, born in Oglethorpe County in 1808, left Auraria for Louisiana in 1833. He served in the legislature of that state and was for a time a judge of the circuit court. He moved to Texas in 1845, settling in San Antonio. In 1857 he was elected to the Texas legislature. He died in 1868. *Ibid.,* II, 344. George Washington Paschal, the most famous of the Paschal brothers, born at Skull Shoals, Georgia, in 1812, left Auraria in helping to remove the Cherokees to Indian Territory. While on that expedition he married Sarah, a daughter of Chief John Ridge. He settled in Arkansas where he was soon elected chief justice of the state supreme court. He moved to Texas in 1847, settling first in Galveston, but later in Austin. He edited here the *Southern Intelligencer,* in which he upheld Sam Houston and the Union. He remained unpopular during the Civil War, using much of his time in preparing the *Digest of the*

Laws of Texas, which was published in 1866. This year he left Texas
for New York and three years later opened a law office in Washington,
D. C. He became a Republican. He was married three times. By his
wife Sarah he had two sons. Next he married Marcia Duval, a daughter
of William P. Duval, territorial governor of Florida (1822-1834). Two
daughters came to this union, one being Mrs. T. P. O'Connor, famous
as the author of *My Beloved South* (New York, 1913). Paschal's third
wife was Mrs. Mary Scoville Harper. He died in 1878 in Washington.
Ibid., II, 343-44.

11. *Southern Banner,* July 8 (3, 1), 1852.
12. *Ibid.*, May 27 (3, 1).
13. Athens *Southern Whig,* February 22 (2, 7), 1849.
14. *Southern Banner,* April 13 (2, 6), 1854.
15. Thomas Baldwin and J. Thomas, *A New and Complete Gazetteer of the United States.* . . . (Philadelphia, 1854), 64.
16. *The Southern Business Directory and General Commercial Advertiser* (Charleston, 1854), I, 263. These merchants were: B. W. Brackett, J. F. Lilly, I. E. Wood, P. E. Willis (postmaster), and E. B. Wells.
17. George White, *Historical Collections of Georgia.* . . . (New York, 1854), 542.
18. Cain, *History of Lumpkin County,* 55-56. According to Mrs. Richard French Spencer, San Antonio, Texas, granddaughter of Oliver Russell, the four Russell brothers (John, Green, Levi, and Oliver) first went to California during the gold-rush years of 1848-1850. Letter to E. M. Coulter, July 20, 1956.
19. *Webster's Geographical Dictionary. A Dictionary of Names of Places with Geographical and Historical Information and Pronounciations* (Springfield, Mass., 1949), 82.
20. Margaret Inman Meaders, "The Perplexing Case of John H. Gregory," in *Georgia Historical Quarterly,* XL, 2 (June, 1956), 113-29.
21. Cain, *History of Lumpkin County,* 143.
22. Paschal, *Agnes Paschal,* 300.
23. *Ibid.*, 295-97.
24. Adiel Sherwood, *A Gazetteer of Georgia.* . . . (Fourth edition. Macon, 1860), 196.
25. Paschal, *Agnes Paschal,* 9, 11, 245-46, 253, 255, 306.
26. "Gold Mining in Georgia," in *Harper's New Monthly Magazine,* LIX (September, 1879), 516-17.
27. Yeates, McCallie, and King, *Preliminary Report,* 265-66. The naming of Auraria is here erroneously attributed to John C. Calhoun.
28. Yates, McCallie, and King, *Preliminary Report,* 484, 524.
29. *Atlanta Constitution,* July 13 (5K, 1), 1930. The Ordinary at this time was A. L. Dorsey.
30. Austin F. Dean, ed., *Observations from a Peak in Lumpkin or the Writings of W. B. Townsend, Editor, The Dahlonega Nugget* (Gainesville, Ga., 1936), 256.
31. *Ibid.*
32. Andrew Sparks, "Is $3,000,000 Buried in a Georgia Cave?," in *Atlanta Journal and Constitution Magazine,* August 16, 1953, pp. 20-22. For evidences of tourism in Dahlonega see John Riley, "There's another Gold Rush in Dahlonega," *ibid.*, September 26, 1954, pp. 10-12; Raleigh Bryans, "The Gold Rush to Dahlonega Pans out Happy Affair," in *Atlanta*

Journal and Atlanta Constitution, October 17 (1, 1-5, Section C), 1954;
T. Conn Bryan, "The Gold Rush in Georgia," in *Georgia Review,* IX, 4
(Winter, 1955), 402-04.

BIBLIOGRAPHY

I. Books

Andrews, Garnett, *Reminiscences of an Old Georgia Lawyer.* Atlanta: Franklin Steam Printing House, 1870.

Blake, William P., *Report upon the Gold Placers of a Part of Lumpkin County, Georgia and the Practicability of Working them by the Hydraulic Method, with Water from the Chestatee River.* New York: John F. Trow, 1858.

Cain, Andrew W., *History of Lumpkin County for the first Hundred Years, 1832-1932.* Atlanta: Stein Printing Co., 1932.

Dykeman, Wilma, *The French Broad.* Volume 49 in Rivers of America Series. New York: Rinehart & Company, Inc., 1955.

Elliott, Charles Winslow, *Winfield Scott. The Soldier and the Man.* New York: The Macmillan Company, 1937.

Hull, A. L., *A Historical Sketch of the University of Georgia.* Atlanta: The Foote & Davies Co., 1894.

Lumpkin, Wilson, *The Removal of the Cherokee Indians from Georgia.* 2 volumes. New York: Dodd Mead & Company, 1907.

Orr, Dorothy, *A History of Education in Georgia.* Chapel Hill: The University of North Carolina Press, 1950.

Paschal, George W., *Ninety-Four Years. Agnes Paschal.* No place: No publishers, 1871. Stereotyped by M'Gill & Witherow, Washington, D. C.

[Simms, William Gilmore,] *Guy Rivers: A Tale of Georgia.*

By the Author of "Martin Faber." 2 volumes. New York: Harper & Brothers, 1834.

Wright, Albert Hazen, *Our Georgia-Florida Frontier. The Okefinokee Swamp, its History and Cartography.* Ithaca, N. Y.: A. H. Wright, 1945.

II. GOVERNMENT PUBLICATIONS

Acts of the General Assembly of the State of Georgia, . . . Annual Session in November and December, 1828. Milledgeville: Camak & Ragland, 1829; *ibid., 1829.* Milledgeville: Camak & Ragland, 1830; *ibid., October, November and December, 1830.* Milledgeville: Camak & Ragland, 1831; *ibid., 1831.* Milledgeville: Prince & Ragland, 1832; *ibid., 1832.* Milledgeville: Prince & Ragland, 1833; *ibid., 1833.* Milledgeville: Polhill & Fort, 1834; *ibid., 1834.* Milledgeville: P. L. & B. H. Robinson, 1835; *ibid., 1857.* Columbus: Tennent Lomax, 1858; *ibid., 1859.* Milledgeville: Boughton, Nisbet & Barnes, 1860; *ibid., Called Session, Beginning July 4, and Ending October 6, 1868.* Macon: J. W. Burke & Co., 1868.

Gold & Land Lottery Register, No. 49. Milledgeville: Federal Union Office, Polhill & Cuthbert, 1833.

Journal of a General Convention of the State of Georgia, to Reduce the Members of the General Assembly. Begun and Held at Milledgeville, the Seat of Government, in May, 1833. Milledgeville: Printed at the Federal Union Office, 1833.

Journal of the Senate of the State of Georgia at the Annual Session of the General Assembly, . . . in November and December, 1834. Milledgeville: P. L. & B. H. Robinson, 1835.

Yeates, W. S., S. W. McCallie, and Francis P. King, *A Preliminary Report on a Part of the Gold Deposits of Georgia.* Bulletin No. 4-A, Geological Survey of Georgia. Atlanta: Geo. W. Harrison, 1896.

III. Maps

Bonner's Map of the State of Georgia with the Addition of its Geological Features. Savannah: W. T. Williams, 1849. Folded and inserted opposite page 28 in George White, *Statistics of the State of Georgia.* For a full bibliographical citation on this work, see Section VI of this Bibliography.

Bonner's Pocket Map of the State of Georgia. Compiled by Wm. G. Bonner, Civil Engineer. Milledgeville, 1851.

Map of the First Section of .that Part of Georgia now Known as the Cherokee Territory in which are Delineated all the Districts and Lots, which by an Act of the General-Assembly were Designated the Gold Districts. And Taken from Actual Survey by Orange Green. Published by Cowles, Daggett, & Co. (No place, no date).

IV. Manuscripts

Minutes of the Antioch Baptist Church in Auraria. These minutes begin with the organization meeting on July 13, 1833 and continue to June 5, 1869. No minutes were entered during the period of the Civil War. This record is in private possession.

Records of the Superior Court of Lumpkin County. There are various records unlabelled for the most part, such as minutes, writs, dockets, etc. They begin with the organization of the county in 1833. (The county was authorized by the legislature in December 1832.) These records are in the Office of the Clerk of the Court, in Dahlonega.

V. Newspapers, Special Articles in Newspapers, and Compilations of Editorials and News Accounts

Athens *Southern Banner,* 1832, 1833, 1852, 1854.
Athens *Southern Whig,* 1849.
Atlanta Constitution, 1930.
Atlanta Journal, 1934.
Auraria *Western Herald,* 1833-1834.

Bryans, Raleigh, "New Gold Rush to Dahlonega Pans out Happy Affair," in *Atlanta Journal and Atlanta Constitution,* October 17, Section C (1-1, 2, 3, 4, 5), 1954.

Dean, Austin F., ed., *Observations from a Peak in Lumpkin or the Writings of W. B. Townsend, Editor, The Dahlonega Nugget.* Printed by Oglethorpe University Press, Oglethorpe University, Ga., and copyrighted in 1936.

New York Herald-Tribune Book Review, 1955.

Riley, John, "There's Another Gold Rush in Dahlonega," in *Atlanta Journal and Constitution Magazine,* September 26, 1954, pp. 10-12.

Savannah *Georgian,* 1834, 1835.

Sparks, Andrew, "Is $3,000,000 Buried in a Georgia Cave?," in *Atlanta Journal and Constitution Magazine,* August 16, 1953, pp. 20-22.

VI. PERIODICALS

Bryan, T. Conn, "The Gold Rush in Georgia," in *Georgia Review.* Volume IX. Athens, 1955.

Christian Index and Baptist Miscellany. Jesse Mercer, ed. Washington, Ga., 1833.

"Gold Mining in Georgia," in *Harper's New Monthly Magazine.* Volume LIX. New York, 1879.

Green, Fletcher M., "Georgia's Forgotten Industry: Gold Mining," Parts I, II in *Georgia Historical Quarterly.* Volume XIX. Savannah, 1935.

Niles' Weekly Register. H. Niles, editor. Volumes XXXIX (1830-1831), XLIV (1833), XLV (1833-1834). Baltimore.

VII. STATISTICAL, ENCYCLOPAEDIC, AND COLLECTED WORKS

American Almanac and Repository of Useful Knowledge, for the Year 1835. Boston: Charles Bowen, 1834.

Baldwin, Thomas, and J. Thomas, *A New and Complete Gazetteer of the United States. . . .* Philadelphia: Lippincott, Grambo & Co., 1854.

Memoirs of Georgia. Containing Historical Accounts of the State's Civil, Military, Industrial and Professional Interests, and Personal Sketches of Many of the People. 2 volumes. Atlanta: The Southern Historical Association, 1895.

Oliphant, Mary C. Simms, Alfred Taylor Odell, and T. C. Duncan Eaves, eds., *The Letters of William Gilmore Simms.* 5 volumes projected. Volume I. Columbia, S. C.: University of South Carolina Press, 1952.

Sherwood, Adiel, *A Gazetteer of Georgia. . . .* Fourth edition. Macon: S. Boykin, 1860.

Sherwood, Adiel, *A Gazetteer of the State of Georgia. . . .* Third edition. Washington, D. C.: P. Force, 1837.

Southern Business Directory and General Commercial Advertiser. Volume I. Charleston, S. C.: Steam Power Press of Walker & James, 1854.

Webb, Walter Prescott *et al.*, eds., *The Handbook of Texas.* 2 vols. Austin: The Texas State Historical Association, 1952.

Webster's Geographical Dictionary. A Dictionary of Names of Places with Geographical and Historical Information and Pronunciations. Springfield, Mass.: G. & C. Merriam Co., 1949.

White, George, *Historical Collections of Georgia: Containing the Most Interesting Facts, Traditions, Biographical Sketches, Anecdotes, etc. Relating to its History and Antiquities, from its First Settlement to the Present Time. . . .* New York: Pudney & Russell, 1854.

White, George, *Statistics of the State of Georgia: Including an Account of its Natural, Civil, and Ecclesiastical History; together with a Particular Description of each County, Notices of the Manners and Customs of its Aboriginal Tribes, and a Correct Map of the State.* Savannah: W. Thorne Williams, 1849.

INDEX

A. M'Laughlin & Company, merchants, 19

Academies, 45-46

Adam, slave runaway, 49

Adams, Henry, judge of Court of Ordinary, 79

Agriculture, 20, 53

Alabama, 73

Alabama River, 7

Albon Chase & Co., newspaper firm, 33

Aldoradda, name suggested for Lumpkin County, 8

Allatoona gold mines, 50

Amicalola, Ga., 77

"Amicus Veri," pen-name, 42, 44

Andrews, Garnett, lawyer, attends court in Auraria, 31; describes conditions in Auraria, 41

Antioch Baptist Church, in Auraria, 124 (n. 17)

Apalachicola, Fla., 73

Apalachicola River, 7

Appleby, John, offers toast at Fourth of July celebration, 91

Apprentices, 51

Arkansas, G. W. Paschal settles in, 110, 130 (n. 10)

Athenian, Athens newspaper, 33

Athens, Ga., 30, 33, 35, 44, 56, 73, 74, 86, 107, 111, 121 (n. 5)

Athens, Tenn., 28, 74

Athens Stage Line, 74

Atlanta Journal, comments on *Western Herald,* 108

Augusta, Ga., 21, 28, 73, 74

Auraria, settled by miners, 7; names suggested, 7-8; name selected, 8; meaning of name, 8, 9; described

in doggerel, 8-9; rapid growth, 16-17; population, 17, 115, 121 (n. 1); in lottery, 17; taverns, 17-18, merchants, 18-21, 131 (n. 16); business methods, 18-19, 22; prices, 20-21, 22; meeting to secure mint, 25; bank meeting, 25-26; branch of Bank of Darien, 26-27; manufactories, 27; tailors, 27-28; barbers, 28-29; doctors, 29; lawyers, 29-31; county seat, 31, 79; orphans' lot, 31-32; town lots set up, 32; description, 32; newspapers, 33-38, 106-109, 110-11; tradition of wickedness, 38-39, 115-16; defense, 39, 58, 115, 116; characteristics, 39, 80; religion, 39-44, 65; graveyard, 40, 68-69, 116; education, 44, 46; crimes, 47-48, 52-54, 115-16; slaves, 50-51, 60; horse-stealing, 52; in Simms' novel, 55, 116; life, 57-72; color line, 58, 59, 60; Christmas, 64, 65; Fourth of July, 65-68; toast to, 67; weddings, 68; deaths, 68-69; frolic, 69-72; geographical location, 73-74; stage connections, 74-77; mail service, 77-78; post office, 77-78; incorporated, 78, 127 (n. 10); city limits, 78; city government, 79-80; health, 80-82, 128 (n. 16, n. 18); visited by a Cherokee, 83; opposed to Federal concentration, 84-94; organizes State Rights Party, 92-93; opposes selection of Dahlonega as county court site, 97-98; loses county offices, 103; uncalled-for mail in post office, 103; decline, 106-17; loses newspaper, 107, 108; gains newspaper, 108; references to decline, 111, 112,